FLATWEAVES
— OF —
TURKEY

FLATWEAVES
— OF —
TURKEY

To Christina,
I hope you enjoy our book.
Robin Brandt

 AREND BANDSMA AND ROBIN BRANDT

CRAWFORD HOUSE PRESS
BATHURST

A CHP Production

Produced by
Crawford House Press Pty Ltd
PO Box 1484
Bathurst NSW 2795 Australia

A joint publication of the Ministry of Culture of the
Republic of Turkey and Crawford House Press Pty Ltd.

Designed by Kylie Ledger

National Library of Australia Cataloguing-in-Publication entry
    Bandsma, A. T. (Arend T.)
       Flatweaves of Turkey

       Bibliography.
       Includes index.
       ISBN 1 86333 079 8

       1. Kilims - Turkey. 2. Textile fabrics - Turkey.
       3. Weaving - Turkey. I. Brandt, R. T. (Robin T.).
       II. Title.

  746.1409561

Printed in Hong Kong by Colorcraft Ltd

10 9 8 7 6 5 4 3 2 1

CONTENTS

FOREWORD

Our fascination with the flatweaves of Turkey began many years ago on our first visit to that country. An interest in tribal hand-knotted rugs had already given us an appreciation of good vegetable dyes.

Seeing the wealth of colour and design of the Turkish flatweaves for the first time had us enthralled. Our enthusiasm soon developed into a passion, reinforced by regular trips back to Turkey. Subsequently, our regard for piled rugs diminished, something we have noted in other collectors, whether they be from Turkey, Europe or America. Piled rugs lack the immediacy of flatweaves, particularly of kilims.

Collecting kilims can assume the proportions of an illness, which many Turkish dealers recognise. One is often introduced to another collector or dealer by the expression, "He is sick too", or, "He is also mad!"

The intrinsic properties of flatweaves (a merging of tradition and art), which so greatly enrich our lives, are perceived by all collectors of these works. On one occasion, one of the authors, while protesting to a dealer that he was only a poor teacher and unable to afford the price of a kilim being offered, was informed emphatically, "You are not poor! You like kilims!"

It is the Turkish weavings we find the most exciting. Although our collection includes some fine old Iranian and Caucasian pieces, generally we find that they lack the splendid variety and innovations found in their Turkish relatives.

Weaving was traditionally the work of women. Their creativity began with their first having to spin and dye the wool. The weavers of the past were obviously very committed to their task, for many of the earlier pieces are intricately designed and woven with finely spun wool. These were not the products of exploited labour – no tortured fingers, no eyes strained to the point of blindness that we hear about in the rug industry of India and Pakistan. Instead, they were a labour of love.

The majority of the flatweaves illustrated in this book date from the 19th century, some from early in the century, others later. Rather than indicate the age each time alongside the plate, we have decided to omit this information, for to write "early 19th century", "first half of the 19th century", and so on, would be repetitive and of little value.

The flatweaves shown have been chosen using the following criteria: they are traditional weavings (that is, they have a cultural significance), possess good natural dyes and have a harmony of design and colour. Their artistry should be self-evident; none are influenced by the degrading aspects that developed with the advent of synthetic dyes and the forces of commerce.

There is a growing element of sophisticated snobbery in the minds of some so-called experts about classifying kilims according to age. They consider pieces woven since 1800 to be insignificant in cultural terms and relegate them to the category of the merely decorative. The search is on for "the fragmentary masterpieces of earlier generations".

The trend is to date pieces earlier and earlier. Battered fragments, providing they contain recognisably good vegetable dyes, are immediately assumed to be of great antiquity. One pities those collectors with dated rugs, because the age of these pieces is finite. Dated pieces, unless the date is very early (and that is extremely rare), are now almost a liability in any collection. While some genuinely old fragments are quite splendid and can augment a collection, one should not reject out of hand all kilims woven since the early 19th century. Many nomadic and tribal groups maintained their cultural identity, and weaving skills, until the 1870s or 1880s. Some kept to their age-old customs well into this century.

Dissatisfaction with some of the repairs done in Turkey led us to attempt our own. We go to the extent of dyeing and spinning wool to match each piece. This has opened up a whole new avenue in our appreciation of these old textiles. Not only have we come to acknowledge at first hand the skill of some of these early spinners and weavers, but our awareness of wool quality, colour harmony and the various techniques has been greatly increased. Doing one's own restoration is very rewarding and something we can recommend, but be warned – it is very intensive work and very time consuming.

In our years of visiting Turkey we have made many good friends. The Turks are a wonderfully hospitable, generous and extremely honest nation of people. Some of our early contacts are no longer in the business because of the dearth of available old pieces, but we still remain on very friendly terms.

We would like to take this opportunity to thank our many friends and contacts in Turkey, from whom we have received so much hospitality and also, over the years, gleaned so much information. Among the many people who have given us encouragement and help to complete this book, Chris Carter and Peter Kaiser are owed a special acknowledgement – Chris for reading through our text and giving invaluable suggestions, and Peter for preparing the map which accompanies the text. We wish also to thank Gerard Benacek for his assistance throughout, in particular for his expertise with the computer, which has been of immense help in organising the material. This book is not meant to be a scholarly treatise on flatweaves, but a vehicle for sharing our enjoyment of these fascinating textiles. We hope that through this work we are able to engender more of an interest in them before this aspect of man's cultural heritage is swallowed up in the uniformity of the modern age. However, for any real appreciation of them it is also essential to have some understanding of the weaving techniques involved and also to be able to relate the weavings to the people who made them. These aspects we have attempted to explain as accurately as possible.

INTRODUCTION

About three times the area of New Zealand or the United Kingdom, Turkey is divided by the Bosporus, Sea of Marmara and the Dardanelles into a European fragment, Thrace (about 3 per cent of the total land mass), and the much larger Asian, or Anatolian portion. Anatolia is a land of high plateaus, rising progressively towards the mountain ranges in the east.

The lofty Taurus Mountains extend along the Mediterranean side, separating a narrow, fertile, coastal strip from the generally more arid interior. Several large and historically significant rivers cut through the Anatolian plateau. These include the Euphrates, Tigris and Meander. Turkey possesses several lakes, of which one, Lake Van, is almost large enough to be called an inland sea. There are also numerous salt lakes and marshes in western and central Anatolia.

The population is composed of two major groups. The larger is of Turkic origin and traces its roots to central Asia. A smaller Kurdish component lives mainly in the east of Turkey. Over the ages, Yörüks, the nomadic Turkic tribesmen, steadily settled down, a process that quickened over the 19th and 20th centuries. Today, Yörüks are mainly confined to the Taurus ranges. The vacuum created as they settled was occupied, to a degree, by the semi-nomadic Kurds, who have gradually extended their range westwards and northwards.

The peoples' movements over the centuries, in association with relocation and settlement, whether forced or voluntary, has led to segmentation of the original tribes, thus making positive determination of the provenance of weavings difficult. Many of the names used to denote kilims are dealers' terms and sometimes bear little relationship to the people or places where they were actually woven. For example, Reyhanli nomads once made extensive migrations to plains south of Sivas in central east Anatolia; the town Reyhanli, on the other hand, lies in the south, close to the Syrian border. So kilims described as Reyhanli are sometimes those with design, colours and workmanship typical of the south, similar to the so-called Aleppo kilims; sometimes they resemble Malatya or Sivas kilims.

While classification is a useful tool in any analysis, it poses difficulties with Turkish weavings because many of the old skills have long been forgotten. Indeed it may be too late to find out exactly which people made some pieces. The common names in use are convenient for a casual categorisation of flatweaves but one must accept that many are inexact and sometimes quite misleading. Consequently, where possible, we have attempted to relate the weavings to the tribal groups who made them. Names of towns, where used, are merely geographical indicators for ease of defining the areas being discussed.

BULGARIA

BLACK SEA

GREECE

THRACE

SEA OF MARMARA

ISTANBUL

∴ Troy

• Bursa

• Çankiri

• Çorum

• Balikesir

Eskişehir • • Sivrihisar • ANKARA

HAYMANA
PLAINS

• Kütahya

A N A T O

• Bergama

• Manisa

Uşak •

• Afyon

Lake
Tuz

• Izmir

MEANDER RIVER

Cihanbeyli •

• Askaray

∴ Ephesus

• Akşehir

OBRUK
PLAINS

• Yah

Aydin •

• Niğde

• Çine

• Denizli

• Dazkiri

T A U R U S

• Konya

• Karapinar

• Muğla

M O U N T A I N S

• Çumra • Hotamiş

TA

• Antalya

Adana •

ÇUKUROV

• Fethiye

• Mut

• Ermenek

Silifke •

TURKEY

MEDITERRANEAN SEA

N

GEORGIA

RUSSIAN FEDERATION

sun •

• Ordu   • Trabzon

                                    • Kars

                                                    ARMENIA

• Tokat

              • Bayburt   • Kağizman   Iğdir •
                                                              Δ
                        • Erzerum   Mount
                                                             Ararat

• Sivas   • Ağri

A
    M
    O
    U
    N
    T
    A
    I
    N
    S
                                                    Lake
                                                    Van

      • Malatya   • Van

                                                              IRAN

                                    • Siirt

                                                                    • Rezaiyeh

      • Adiyaman   Diyarbakir •
                                              • Hakkari
• Maraş

• Gaziantep
              • Urfa   • Irbil

eyhanli •

  • Aleppo
                    E U P H R A T E S   R I V E R

                                                    T
                                                    I
                                                    G
                                                    R
                                                    I
                                                    S
                                                        R
                                                        I
                                                        V
                                                        E
                                                        R
                                                                    IRAQ

SYRIA

PART onE

FIGURE 1: *Yörük people breaking camp in preparation for their day's trek through the Taurus Mountains towards their winter grazing grounds, October 1992. Note the decorative çuvals.*

MAN AND TEXTILES

An interest in textiles probably began from the time that humans first learnt to twist or braid materials together. To begin with, the products would have been utilitarian – used for clothing, shelter and hunting. Being creative artists, people tended to decorate even the most mundane of objects; experimentation with different techniques and colours obtained from their surroundings would have followed as a natural course and led to further development of their skills.

Early associations with animals meant that wool and hair were among the first materials to be used in spinning and weaving. Sheep are known to have been domesticated about 9000 BC in south-west Asia. Along with numerous stone spinning whorls, knives of the same type used by modern-day Turkoman women to cut the yarn while making piled rugs have been recovered from several women's graves in southern Turkmenia. These date back to the 14th century BC. This would suggest that already in the Bronze Age, rug making was a firmly established craft.

The oldest hand-woven materials are known from very fragmentary remains found at Çatalhüyük, south of Konya. These date from around 6500 BC. Cotton also has had a long history of use, not only in the East, but as far away as South America. Patterned textiles from as long ago as 2500 BC have been found there. Although in these early American materials the cotton fibres were merely twined together, the designs point to artisans with well-developed creative abilities.

Apart from their useful and decorative purposes, textiles, at a very early stage, began to assume a deeper significance in the lives of the people who wove them. Underlying their artistic inventiveness were often designs reflecting culture and religion. Fabrics also played a part in the development of the architecture of some societies. Designs first woven into materials were later copied on buildings.

Weavings came to be regarded as valued possessions. This is seen in the role they played as burial accompaniments in funerary rites. In 1949 the Russian archaeologist Rudenko excavated some Scythian burial mounds at Pazyryk, in a glacial valley in the Altai Mountains of southern Siberia. He unearthed several textiles from the grave of what was almost certainly a chieftain who died about 400 BC. One of these textiles, now known as the Pazyryk carpet, is a piled rug with a field drawn up in squares, and depicts elks and men on horseback in its borders. It has about thirty-six symmetrical ("Turkish") knots per square centimetre. It is predominantly red, blue, yellow, green and orange – that is, it contains all the basic colours used in more recent weavings. Tapestry weaves and ornamented felts were also found at Pazyryk.

Predating the Pazyryk find is a fragment of a saddle cover which Rudenko later unearthed at Bashadar, 180 kilometres west of Pazyryk. Approximately 130 years older than the Pazyryk carpet, it is very finely woven with about seventy asymmetrical ("Persian") knots to the square centimetre.

These early fabrics from Siberia illustrate not only that both knotting methods used in more modern rugs have a long history, but also that weaving skills, including the extraction of dyes, were already then highly developed. It can be safely assumed that kilims and other flatweaves, assuredly forerunners of the piled carpet technique, were by then thoroughly integrated in the lives and art form of those peoples. What is less well known about the Pazyryk finds is that one of the burial mounds contained fragments of a slit-tapestry kilim weave used as a trim for red woollen cloth. Made of woollen warps and wefts, it had a composition consisting of rows of reciprocal hooks worked in red, blue, yellow, white and maroon. This attractive textile must have taken the fancy of grave robbers, because they tore most of the kilim weave away but left the larger red fabric – surely the earliest recorded theft of a kilim!

It is obvious that the weavings found at Pazyryk and Bashadar were considered important, for they were buried alongside the chieftain's favourite possessions – his wives, horses, saddles, harnesses, woodcarvings, bronze vessels used in hashish rituals, and so on.

That these objects, and mummified bodies which they accompanied, survived until the present was brought about by a quirk of fate. Grave robbers, while searching for gold, jewellery and other valuable items not long after the mounds were formed, excavated passages that allowed water to enter the sites; the permafrost subsequently froze all the objects in the graves in a mantle of ice, thus preserving them perfectly until they were rediscovered this century.

The burial mounds that Rudenko and his fellow archaeologists explored were at high altitudes in the mountains. Burials could only have been carried out in the summer, so the bodies of chiefs who died at other times of the year would have had to be preserved until the nomads returned to their alpine pasture lands. (Some of the recovered bodies showed evidence of mummification, a process which involved removing the entrails and replacing them with herbs). These areas, remote from attack, became the sanctuaries of the Turks, Mongols and other nomads, places where groups reunited and recovered their strength after winter struggles in the lowlands against other tribes. The mountain refuges came to be looked upon as the spiritual home of the nomads – the place to settle differences, arrange marriages and be buried.

Present-day nomads, while steadily diminishing in numbers through the attempts of the home governments to settle them and because of the allure of the luxuries of modern life, still retain this deep-set yearning for their mountain homelands.

About the same time that the Pazyryk and Bashadar burial mounds were being formed, some cultures in South America were also weaving imaginatively designed and brightly coloured fabrics. Executed in plain kilim or brocaded technique, many of these weavings depict, in vibrant colour, extraordinary representations of men and animals. Most surviving pieces are grave cloths recovered from the dry desert land of Peru. In this region, materials and dyes have remained in a good state because of the exceptional aridity of the Peruvian deserts, where in some parts there has been little or no rain over millennia.

In those areas of the globe where extreme seasonal differences in temperature and rainfall had a regulatory effect on vegetation, nomadism followed the domestication of animals as a natural course. Herdsmen had to seek new pastures for their burgeoning flocks. In parts, from the Middle East to Mongolia, a seasonal pattern emerged. Flocks were grazed on lowland pastures during the winter months, but as those lands became parched with the onset of summer, the animals were moved to the mountain slopes. When the autumn snows began to fall they were driven back down again. As populations of both man and beasts grew, conflicts over grazing and water rights became inevitable. It was the result of these pressures that saw Anatolia settled by Turkic people.

Little is known about the early history of the Turkomans. For many centuries they ranged the huge steppes and mountains of southern Siberia and Sinkiang, from the edges of the Gobi to the Caspian Sea. Most of these areas are still predominantly Turkic and the people for the main part are of nomadic stock.

Beginning with the Selçuk Turks about 900 years ago, waves of Turks began to occupy what is modern-day Turkey. Turkoman and Muslim influences were transferred from the Khorasan homeland to Anatolia. Konya became the capital of the Selçuk state. In the early part of the 13th century, under Genghis Khan, and again in the 15th century, under Tamerlane, the expanding Mongol forces drove further Turkic tribes westwards into Asia Minor. These migrations have continued spasmodically until the present day, with new migrants from the Caucasus and Crimea in the 19th and early 20th centuries, as Russia extended her influence, and from the Balkan states when they were lost by the Ottoman Empire. Turkish speaking people from Afghanistan, refugees resulting from the Soviet invasion of that country, and Bulgarian Turks are the most recent wave to reach Turkey.

It can be supposed that before the arrival of the Turks there was already a thriving weaving industry in Asia Minor. When the various tribes began to settle in different parts of their new homeland the invading culture absorbed and dominated the indigenous one. The design of the tribal emblems, or güls, was retained, but now produced in the materials and colours of the new environment. These distinctive motifs can still be seen, especially in the storage bags of many tribes – see, for example, plates 74, 76 and 77. New patterns were developed as individual villages and subtribes emerged, but underlying all was their strong association with the Khorasan. Even today, many seemingly sophisticated and Western-oriented Turks talk, with both nostalgia and enthusiasm, about their ancestral home and their links with the past.

Looking at a map of Turkey, one can see that many towns and villages bear the names of various tribes or places from their previous homelands. Quite a large sector of the population resisted settling down and instead clung to traditional nomadic ways. The lifestyle of this group of people bears further examination because it is reflected in their weavings and has a very strong influence on those in outlying villages.

Nomads scorn a settled existence with its concomitant accumulation of luxuries. They require a few bare necessities and, for the rest, prefer to remain free in spirit, leading their flocks over the annual migratory routes. The harsh conditions of their environment, coupled with the need to defend themselves against others, meant that tribal organisation was very important. They accepted the authority of their chiefs but otherwise often did not recognise central government. This, of course, led to numerous clashes with government forces, which over centuries saw nomadic groups forcibly settled in villages, split up and transposed and, in some cases, annihilated.

Towards the end of last century the Ottoman rulers made efforts to settle the nomads throughout Turkey. The government had no time for people who did not pay taxes or supply men for the army. The Yörüks of the Taurus Mountains in south-west Turkey were particularly harshly treated. These nomads resisted the yoke that the government was trying to impose and in 1876 heavy fighting broke out between them and the Ottoman armed forces. Faced with superior numbers and weapons, the Yörüks were ultimately defeated, despite having fought valiantly. The army closed off the mountain passes, thus preventing the remnants of the nomadic tribes from pursuing their seasonal migrations. Many were forced to settle on the Çukurova Plains, where, devoid of the cool, clear mountain air, they suffered from the summer heat and humidity. Malaria and other diseases decimated them; local government officials bullied, cheated and mentally broke them. Very little assistance was offered to train them in agricultural practices. By bribing the guards at the mountain passes a few managed to slip back and rejoin the scattered groups remaining in their mountain refuges. Yashar Kemal, particularly in *The Legend of the Thousand Bulls*, portrays these times vividly. Many nomadic tribes in other parts of the Taurus Mountains and in the north-west of Anatolia suffered a similar fate.

Before the Ottoman policy of enforced resettlement, there used to be encampments of hundreds of black goat-hair tents in the Taurus Mountains. Today one is fortunate to see as many as twenty together. More often there are groups of at most half a dozen tents. Still, there is a resilience and strength of spirit in those nomads who remain, despite the increasing difficulties in obtaining winter pasturage as more and more land becomes settled and turned under the plough. They regard themselves as the real people.

In Iran the Qashgais had their own problems with the central government. They are a Turkic group of people who probably remained behind in Azerbaijan following the Selçuk invasions. In the 13th century, they moved from there to the province of Fars, in south-west Iran. In the 1920s, Reza Shah, the father of the last shah, began a military operation against them in an effort to stamp out their nomadic lifestyle. After defeating and disarming these freedom-loving nomads the shah organised large settlement schemes. Until 1941, when Reza Shah abdicated, this enforced settlement was executed in such a ruthless manner that many Qashgais succumbed to diseases and starvation. A great number were settled in the lowlands, where they found the scorching summer heat unbearable; others were cut off in the mountains, unable to return to their winter lowland pastures. After 1941, when the government eased the pressure, many of the Qashgais went back to their nomadic life. However, interference by the state continues and during the last decades their summer and winter migrations have been kept under strict control.

Another group of tribesmen to have felt the ire of central government are the Afshars. Also Turkic in origin, they, like the Qashgais, settled in Persian Azerbaijan, where they became a very powerful group. These independent-minded nomads gave the Persian shahs so much trouble that in the 16th century they were forcibly relocated in the south. Today they are mainly settled people, occupying villages and towns.

What is always impressive about meeting nomads, whether they be Yörüks of Turkey or Afghan tribesmen, is their fierce dignity, their independence, their scorn for settled people and their pride in the feats of their ancestors, especially in battle. In spite of their rigorous life, they are usually friendly and extremely hospitable. That their fierceness is not just romantic nonsense is shown by the records of their courage in the frequent battles they had to fight against government armies who have tried to subjugate them, or against other groups of marauding tribespeople. To die in battle was, and still is, honourable. During periods of their history it was the most likely way to leave the world. The essence of the arduous life and struggles of these people is reflected in their tribal sagas, their epic songs and their weavings.

The Kurds, who occupy the eastern regions of Turkey as well as the western part of Iran and northern Iraq, are also people with a tremendous spirit. They are Indo-European, unlike the Turks, who belong to the Altaic group. Semi-nomads, they graze their flocks in the mountain pastures during the summer but retreat to villages for the winter months. Many have also continued to resist the authority of central government.

Their semi-settled existence and long association with their particular environment has an influence on their weavings. These are often intricately designed and subtly coloured, using many intermediate shades, unlike Yörük weavings, which contain vigorous motifs with a bolder and more basic colouration.

As a broad generalisation, weavings can be placed in three categories: workshop or manufactory rugs of cities and towns, home industry rugs of smaller towns and villages, and tribal or nomadic rugs. The first consists of purely commercial rugs, the product of workshops where several looms are set up under the direction of a master weaver or controller. The weavers are employed on a wage-earning basis. Looms, dyed wool and utensils are supplied by the workshop owners. The weavers work from cartoons – squared paper on which the design of the rug is carefully worked out. The ground weave is often cotton or occasionally silk.

While many of these products are fine and perfectly executed, they lack true artistic merit because they are devoid of individualism. Historically, much of this industry was greatly influenced by the courts; more recently, large numbers of workshop rugs have been woven specifically for Western markets.

The relationship between village and tribal rugs is often strong. While the women weave piled rugs for sale, they are not subjected to the same influences as the town or city weavers. Instead, although they may weave to order, they are able to exert a degree of control over the design, materials and colours. Traditional methods remain particularly strong among those villagers more recently settled, or those who retain close links with nomadic groups. Of all the products that come off the loom, flatweaves are the most traditional, for until very recently they were seldom woven for sale. Some villages, settled by people from different tribes, produced several distinct kilim designs, each reflecting the design and weaving skills of their particular group.

One major difference between a modern pile rug such as a Hereke, produced in a workshop, and a tribal kilim is that whereas in the former the weaver has minimal control over the finished product, in the latter she can regulate all stages of its manufacture, from the spinning and dyeing of the materials to the completed article. Drawing from the knowledge and experience gained from the time she was a young girl sitting beside her mother, aunts and grandmother, where techniques, designs and colour combinations became totally assimilated, she is able to create in a process that flows directly from mind to hand. She can do this without first resorting to planning the article on paper. Although based on designs which have been handed down through the generations, each kilim contains the flair and idiosyncrasies of the creator. Kilims can thus be thought of as a true art form.

Unfortunately, over the last twenty or thirty years commercial aspects have entered the field of kilim weaving. Today one finds large numbers of drearily designed, poorly executed and often brashly coloured kilims, which neither conform to traditional weaves from any specific area nor have any artistic qualities.

Dating: Occasionally dates are woven into flatweaves, more particularly in prayer kilims from north-east Turkey. While the date may give the exact age of a piece, one must also consider that the weaver may have copied it from an earlier weaving. Therefore the materials, colour and weaving methods must also be taken into account when attempting to determine the age of a kilim.

Dates are sometimes very difficult to decipher. Most weavers were illiterate and perhaps merely copied the figures supplied by the village scribe. For this reason, numerals were often imprecisely drawn.

The numerals are usually in Arabic. They read as follows:

Most dated kilims follow the Islamic calendar, which begins with Mohammed's flight, the Hegira, from Mecca to Medina in July of AD 622. In older weavings, the dates are based on the lunar year, which is shorter than the solar year of our system. The lunar year gains one year every 33.7 solar years.

Thus, in converting Islamic dates to our system, one must first add 622 and then subtract from this figure the result of dividing the given date by 33.7. For example, **١٢٦٨** reads 1268:

step 1: 1268 + 622 = 1890

step 2: 1268 ÷ 33.7 = 37.6 (say 38)

step 3: 1890 − 38 = AD 1852

An easier but slightly less precise method is simply to add 583 to the Islamic date. For example:

1268 + 583 = AD 1851.

For weavings of the middle to late 19th century the latter method gives results accurate to within one or two years, but the inaccuracy increases with older or more recent ones.

Since 1928, when Kemal Atatürk replaced the Arabic alphabet with the Latin one, dated kilims have used the numeral system and the Gregorian calendar that we employ.

So how does one determine the age of an undated weaving? Comparison with a dated piece of the same type and from the same region can give a fairly good idea. For the rest, the collector must rely on his experience with colour quality, materials and development of design. Conclusions, at best, are of course very subjective.

FIGURE 2: *Yörük child readied for a day's trek through the Taurus Mountains, October 1992.*

FLATWEAVES AND THEIR USES

Flatweaves are quite different in their manufacture to piled rugs. Whereas in piled rugs the designs are created by knots of different colours, the majority of flatweaves are weft-faced – that is, the motifs are formed by inserting variously coloured wefts between the warps. A variety of techniques is employed, as we will describe later. More rarely one encounters warp-faced flatweaves; in these, an assortment of warps of different colours is picked out by the wefts to develop the design.

For the nomadic and village peoples of the Middle East, flatweaves have assumed an important role in their lives for millennia, probably for almost as long as sheep and goats have been domesticated. They were at the same time utilitarian and an expression of their artistic abilities and tribal identity.

Flatweaves were woven for a variety of uses: floor coverings, bed and seat covers, donkey and camel bags, storage bags, cushions, tent decorations, and so on. The finest of them, often dowry pieces, were highly esteemed, to be displayed only on special occasions such as weddings, births and circumcision ceremonies. Certain kilims were used as funeral cloths in which to wrap the body before burial; usually large single-piece weavings, these kilims were retained by the family for this specialised function. Some flatweaves were so skilfully woven, the culmination of years of practice by the weaver, that although they may have had a fundamental functional purpose, such as for a storage bag or prayer mat, they were recognised by the weaver's family as being too good to be used as such. These heirlooms often remained in mint condition as they were handed down from generation to generation.

Even the black tents typical of the nomads ranging from Morocco through the Arab countries, Turkey, Iran, Turkestan and into Afghanistan are woven from wool or goat hair using a plain flatweave technique. Picture such a tent – the floor is covered by one or two large weavings; ranged along one side of the tent are various-sized flat-woven storage bags made from wool or hair, mostly ornately embellished with strong tribal motifs. Over the bags are thrown some decorative flat-woven rugs. To the rear of the tent may be seen a large chest, perhaps the only item of hard furniture in the family's possession. Inside it are kept the dowry items and other family treasures. To complete the scene, a few bolster-like cushions lie scattered about, while hanging from the tent poles are some small bags, also finely worked in a flatweave technique, for storing kitchen utensils or other items.

Essentially, flatweaves are an inseparable part of the nomadic lifestyle, and as such are an expression of its traditions.

Of all the weaving areas of the Middle East, Turkey possesses the greatest variety of traditional and innovative flatweave designs, coupled with the most imaginative use of colour. Each tribal offshoot has its own distinctive designs, although movements of the people over the ages have led to some merging, with the motifs of one region appearing in the weavings of another.

Until recently flatweaves were largely ignored in the West, even by collectors. There are several reasons for this. First, most people want floor rugs, for which piled rugs are more suited than flatweaves. At a very early stage, piled rugs became items of commerce and were woven by women to raise money for the family. Demand stimulated trade, so by the middle of last century manufactories, in which large numbers of piled rugs were produced specifically for Western markets, were set up in many weaving areas. Until very recently flatweaves were not caught up in this world of commerce but retained their purely traditional form.

The growing interest in flatweaves could be attributed to a change in taste in the decor of the modern home; the tribal weaving, with its bolder designs and colours, has become, in many instances, an important element in interior furnishing. The interest in flatweaves is further sponsored by a growing awareness of the cultures of different ethnic groups.

It is ironic that while television can show us this diversity, it is at the same time one of the prime causes of the levelling of cultures. Even as we are apprised of the lifestyles of isolated ethnic groups which have so enriched our species, they are fast being drawn into the oneness of modern life. The flatweaves of Turkey are an art form that is illustrative of the strong tribal identities of the past. It is important that we preserve and appreciate their uniqueness before this aspect of man's cultural heritage also disappears.

It remains to be stated that most flatweaves are better suited to be used as wall-hangings than floor furnishings, as they cannot take the punishment that piled rugs can. A fine old weaving will grace the wall of any home and can possess much more artistic merit than a third-rate painting. And who, today, can afford a second-rate painting, let alone a Rembrandt or a van Gogh?

In many areas the marriage prospects of the young women depended for a great part on their weaving ability. In parts of Turkey, when a girl attained marriageable age her weavings were displayed at the entrance of the tent or the house. Interested suitors would first critically examine her work before discussing the marriage terms with her parents. It was the custom among many nomadic and village people of Turkey for the bride to present her finest weavings to her husband at the time of the wedding. It was said that a man could judge the character of his bride from her work.

Still, one wonders what motivated a woman to sit before her loom for countless hours to produce weavings that were sometimes too flimsy and, besides, too precious to be used as floor coverings, and often too large to be used as wall-hangings in the small dwelling.

Until recently, with the rapid disintegration of the traditional way of life following social reform, the erosion of cultural barriers, and other influences such as radio and television, flatweaves were rarely sold. When roads began to penetrate into previously remote areas, the closed economic unit of the village was subjected to pressures by the breakdown of the family group, as members migrated to cities or even foreign countries to seek work. Since the end of the 19th century, the traditions and skills associated with weaving have been steadily lost as women find they no longer have the time or desire to weave.

Today, Turkish television is full of advertisements for factory-made carpets. The pressure of commercialism on the young family drives it to modernise by replacing old rugs in the home with new manufactory products. Many rug dealers have as their agents men who go from village to village selling machine-made carpets; they often obtain fine old weavings as part of the deal. Other pieces are finding their way into the bazaars because those few nomads who still pursue their traditional way of life are finding it increasingly difficult to pay for winter pastures. As a result, they occasionally have to sacrifice some of their treasured heirlooms.

After having collected in Turkey for many years, we were amazed to find on one particular trip, in four different places, four fine old weavings of a type we had rarely seen. When we expressed our astonishment to a knowledgeable dealer in Konya, who knew the village where the weavings originated, we learnt that a severe drought the previous year had devastated the villagers' crops. Many families had been forced to sell some of their most valued possessions. "But," he added, "you can be sure those families would have been sad for weeks after parting with them." (See plate 38.)

Of course, not all flatweaves have a cultural or an artistic significance. One must presume that in the past, even using good materials and natural dyes, many poorer weavings must have been produced. Of the old pieces that remain, most are the work of skilled weavers. It is for this very reason that they have been preserved. Occasionally, however, one finds a poorly designed or badly woven older piece.

Over the last few decades, when they realised that there was money to be gained from flatweaves, weavers began to produce hurriedly woven and very uninteresting pieces. Stacks of them are available in the rug shops throughout Turkey. Traditions have been trampled on as the weavers borrow designs from other areas and take shortcuts in the weaving process. The wool is usually lustreless and lacking character, no longer carefully selected as in the past, and the colour combinations poor. Gone is the sense of colour harmony, passed down through centuries of experience with natural dyes, that the earlier village or nomad weaver possessed. Instead, the modern weavings often have harsh, chromatic colours, in many cases of poor quality, which often run or fade dramatically after a few years. Now that rank commercialism has taken over flatweave production, who today has the time or the patience to recreate the finely executed pieces of the past, with their intricate designs and infinite variations?

Nowadays, good old weavings with natural colours are becoming increasingly hard to find. Of those available, many have, or require, large amounts of repair and are exorbitantly priced. As one wanders through the bazaars of Istanbul or other major centres, one can see stacks of what are now called "normal" pieces – that is, pieces for the tourist trade. Many of these are faded and washed out and are passed off as antiques. Step inside a shop and see the face of the shopkeeper light up in the expectation of making a sale. If one merely asks for old pieces, one is subjected to an exhausting array of dreary weavings, ranging from garishly coloured new ones with poorly executed designs, to the drab and prematurely old, which have been aged by sunning them. However, ask for *kök boya* (plant dyes) and see the crestfallen look appear on his face with the prospect of the tourist dollars walking out the door again, as he almost always replies in the negative. At present, only a few dealers carry a limited stock of old weavings with vegetable colours, and even then the purchaser has to be wary of the made-up fragments. Some large pieces are even cut into two or three parts which, with the addition of new end borders, are sold as complete articles.

The bags (çuvals) and cushions (yastiks) which furnished the nomads' tents deserve special mention. They are among the most splendid of all weavings and are very worthy additions to any collection.

Our word "bag" has an unpleasant ring to it, as well as connotations of an object with mere menial functions. It tends to degrade these weavings and to detract from the esteem to which they are rightfully entitled. Apart from their sheer aesthetic qualities, many are very skilfully woven, and all known weaving techniques can be found in various bags. In fact, in terms of time and effort alone, some would have required a far greater dedication on the part of the weaver than many significantly larger kilims. They are usually very sturdy textiles, tightly woven, with a large number of warps per lineal measure and with wefts firmly beaten down.

Goat hair, or a mixture of goat hair and wool, was frequently used by Turkmen Yörüks as well as the Kurds for the warps of their storage bags. The weft material is usually wool, but white cotton is commonly used to fill in the areas around the tribal güls to make them stand out clearly – for the nomads are very proud people and the feeling of tribal identity is very important to them. During their migrations, when the bags are strapped to the sides of a camel or donkey, others can see their tribal emblems from afar and so determine to which group the migrants belong.

The bags, of course, spend much of their time inside the tent, where they are used to store clothing, bedding, food and other items. Even here they are displayed prominently, being arranged so that their decorations can be seen clearly from the tent opening. Metallic thread is sometimes used to highlight certain areas of design; occasionally small touches of silk are inserted, and one can find bags further embellished with tufts of dyed mohair or with beads or shells.

The straps used to bind the bags together across the backs of the pack animals are usually, for strength, of goat-hair foundation. Using a warp-faced technique, they often merit individual attention, for they can be beautifully made and intricately designed (see fig. 16).

The amount of material that goes into making a bag should not be underestimated. An ordinary çuval can weigh 2 to 3 kilograms, while large heybes (saddlebags) can weigh much more. Although not the heaviest heybe in our collection, the piece shown in plate 87, for instance, weighs 5.5 kilograms. Its dimensions in its made-up form give a totally false impression of the quantity of material that was required to make it. Woven in one piece on a horizontal loom and later folded and joined along the sides to make the double bags, it would have been an impressive 3.5 metres in length while stretched out on the loom.

A significant reason why the intrinsic qualities of bags should be recognised is that the strength of tribal design and custom was probably kept more alive, and for longer, in the weaving of them than in any other type of woven artefact. Thus, while admiring a bag, we are looking at the longest surviving remnants of a cultural identity as it exists in its purest form. Added to this is the beauty and skill put into the weaving of many of the old pieces, which, battered as they may be by several generations of use, can still offer so much pleasure. Draped over a table or chair, or mounted on a wall, they can look very impressive and are, at once, a statement of artistry and tradition.

Consider the small bag from the Malatya area, in plate 84. Woven mainly of finely spun wool, it also possesses areas worked with metallic thread and others worked with cotton. It has an immediate appeal through its balanced design, complete with borders, and its use of harmonious colours. It is like a large piece in miniature. Large kilims can be impressive because of their sheer size and their capacity to include bold designs and large splashes of colour. In this bag, one appreciates instead the care and attention devoted to the drawing of the fine designs.

The yastiks, such as those in plates 48, 49 and 85, are likewise deserving of attention. Yastiks need not be woven to such robust standards as storage bags. They are often finely and beautifully made and, as is the case with bags, a variety of weaving techniques is used for their manufacture. Similarly, they bear certain designs which are not found in larger weavings from the same area.

MATERIALS

Wool is ideally suited for weaving. It is a strong and resilient fibre and absorbs and retains dyes readily. In the absence of heavy furniture, woollen fabrics made up the majority of the furnishing of the nomad's tent or the villager's hut. The additional properties of warmth, comfort and protectiveness meant that it also provided much of the clothing. Of particular value to the tribesmen living in the cold mountainous areas ranging from Mongolia to Turkey is the fact that it can be felted easily to make their yürts, the characteristic domed tents of these people.

Hair, from goats in particular, has also been widely used in weaving. In Turkey, even today, the production of goat hair for local use is on quite a large scale. It outstrips the production of mohair but has no organised market. The black goats from around Antalya are renowned for the quality of their hair.

Hair is stronger and less elastic than wool and does not shrink like the latter. These qualities, combined with its stiffness, make it a very suitable material for making storage bags. The woven or plaited straps, the herdsman's counterpart of rope, are also often made from hair.

The warps of some tribal rugs are made of hair, or a mixture of hair and wool, but for the facing material it is more difficult to obtain a fine thread. Thus, one has to admire the skill of the weavers of the past who could attain such remarkably thin wefts from such robust material (see plates 5 and 92). Strangely, although Turkey is the home of Angora goats, mohair is rarely used in its pure form in rug weaving, except to highlight some areas or occasionally for warps. Natural, undyed camel hair, the soft lustrous layer next to the camel's body, is sometimes combed out for use as the weft-facing material of kilims and, on occasions, for the pile of knotted rugs.

The surface of wool fibres is covered with minute scales which lie with their free ends towards the tip. Unlike human hair, where the greater part of each scale is overlapped by the next, the scales of wool fibres are fairly free, with about five-sixths of each visible externally. A major difference between wool and hair is that, whereas wool fibres are solid, hairs have a hollow central canal.

Cotton cultivation is dependent on a more settled, agricultural lifestyle. It is extensively grown in the Middle East and is commonly used for the warps and sometimes also for the wefts of piled rugs. The white design areas of flatweaves are frequently of cotton, since it remains white and does not discolour with age and smoke, as does wool. With time and use, the cotton in these areas tends to mat together.

As a material for the pile of knotted rugs, cotton is not as suitable as wool. Since the turn of the century, however, manufactories in Turkey and Iran have produced large numbers of rugs with a pile of mercerised cotton. Often sold under the name of artificial silk, mercerised cotton has a lustre imparted to it during its treatment with caustic solutions.

Although initially strong, it tends to become brittle with age. Consequently, rugs made of this material have relatively short lifetimes.

Pure silk rugs are often associated with finely woven court pieces. Silk is rarely used in flatweaves except very occasionally to highlight certain areas. The fibres are inelastic and have a greater tensile strength than wool, properties which make silk an excellent material for warps. As the cut ends of the fibres are very brittle, silk tends to wear quickly when used for the pile of knotted rugs. In older mixed wool and silk rugs this feature is very noticeable; whereas the woollen parts usually remain quite thick, the silk regions are often worn down to the foundation warps and wefts. Silk lacks the warmth of wool, both in its feel and modulations of colour. Moreover, dye penetration is poorer than in wool and the colours are more transient. While it may be a suitable medium to demonstrate the prowess of the weaver, for it lends itself to intricately designed and finely knotted pieces, silk does not possess those intrinsic properties of wool sought after by most rug collectors.

To distinguish one material from another a combination of burning tests and microscopic examination is necessary. When burnt, wool and hair shrivel and char, emitting a characteristic smell. Cotton smoulders as it burns, powdering away to a loose, fine ash. Instead of the pungent odour of scorched wool or hair, it releases an aroma reminiscent of burning leaves. A burning test on silk gives results similar to wool or hair.

The quality of a fleece depends on several factors such as the breed of the sheep, its age and sex, the nature of the pasture, where it is grazed and climatic factors. Considerable variation occurs on different parts of the animal itself; wool taken from the neck, shoulders and flanks is generally better than from other parts of the sheep. The season of shearing also has an effect on quality, spring-shorn wool being considered superior to autumn wool. The lustre of wool is dependent on the surface structure of the fibres, their size and straightness, and the pattern of the scales.

Today in Turkey, with the emphasis on mechanised agriculture, many areas of formerly good pasture land have been converted to cropping. As a result, many flocks have been relegated to poorer grazing grounds in forested areas, or left to browse on the verges of the cultivated fields, or on the village common – areas which have not received supplementary fertiliser in the hundreds of years that they have been grazed. This substandard fodder, coupled with poor husbandry methods and a decline in the genetics of the breeding stock, is having a marked effect on the quality of wool available at present. In broad terms, less than 50 per cent of a Turkish fleece can be considered usable fibre, compared with more than 90 per cent for New Zealand wools – this does not, however, prevent producers of modern rugs from retaining as much of the fleece as possible, including frass and rubbish, in order to maintain the weight and reduce costs.

Generally, the wool used in the traditional weaving areas contains stronger fibres than the average New Zealand or Australian breed of sheep. It compares more closely to English and Border Leicester, or Scottish Blackface. This is why the modern production of India or Pakistan, which largely relies on fine New Zealand and Australian wools, results in rugs with a character different from the classical types. Similarly, anyone who has attempted to repair a rug with wools commercially available in the West, where the strong fibres have been selectively bred out of the sheep, will have experienced the problems of trying to match the quality and texture of the original.

After being shorn, the fleece is washed to remove dirt and excess oils, then dried and sorted. Before spinning the wool, the weaver customarily combed it. A typical comb comprises long and sturdy metal teeth, whose bases are embedded in a block of wood. The comb is held between the knees while being used and the fleece is drawn through the teeth. Combing organises the wool fibres so that they lie in the same direction and, since all short pieces are removed in the process, the yarn, when spun, is smooth and lustrous, with good light-reflecting properties. Carded wool, on the other hand, produces softer and fuzzier yarn because not all fibres lie parallel to each other. Combed wool is ideal for the manufacture of kilims and piled rugs, carded wool for clothing and blankets.

Traditionally, spinning was carried out using a simple drop spindle. There are two common types. One is shaped like a wooden top with a long axis; the other is in the form of a cross at the end of a long shaft. From a coil of wool wrapped round one arm, a strand is attached to the spindle, which the woman sets in motion with a quick twist of her fingers or by rolling it along her thigh. As the spindle rotates, further wool is pinched off between finger and thumb to extend the thread. The tightness of the spin is controlled by the pressure exerted by her fingers. With this simple device the spinner is able to produce an extraordinarily fine thread, sometimes comparable in thickness to ordinary sewing cotton.

By plying the strands of spun yarn, a stronger thread is produced. For warp material, which needs to be especially strong to withstand the vigorous beating applied during weaving, two, three, or occasionally four strands of wool are twisted together. The weft-facing material of flatweaves is sometimes two plied but more usually unplied. Since some tribal groups characteristically use plied wefts and others unplied, this feature can be used, in combination with other factors, to help determine the provenance of a weaving.

THE LOOM: Far from being a complicated mechanism of beams and braces, complete with tensioning devices and systems for inserting the threads, the nomad's loom is little more than two beams pegged to the ground at the desired distance apart. The warps are stretched between the beams. To facilitate insertion of the wefts, a rod can be passed through the warps, separating alternate ones into upper and lower sets. The lower set is usually attached by cords to another batten, the heddle rod, which is suspended above the warps between two rocks, or else is maintained in its position by a tripod of sticks. When the heddle rod is drawn forwards it raises the lower set of warps above the other, thus allowing a reverse weft to be passed through easily.

If the weaver wishes to halt her work, for reasons of migration or other cause, the loom is easily dismantled. The incomplete weaving is wrapped around the end beams. On reassembling, however, it is often difficult to procure uniform tension on the warps. Consequently, nomadic weavings are frequently characterised by having variations in dimensions and tightness of weave.

The end beams of the looms are usually quite short so that the weavers do not have to carry heavy timbers from place to place. This sets limits on the width of the weaving. Wider kilims are frequently made of two or more pieces joined together. Of course, length is no real problem when working with a horizontal loom; some nomadic kilims are 5 metres or more long.

Village weavers usually set up a vertical loom. It differs very little from the nomad's horizontal type except for a stout pole on either side to hold the end beams apart. The weaver sits before her loom on a bench which she must raise as the weaving progresses. More sophisticated looms allow the end beams to rotate, so that the weaver can roll the completed section of her work around the lower member to maintain a constant working height.

Apart from her deft fingers and a knife, the only other instrument the weaver requires is a beating comb – a heavy metal or wooden tool with long teeth for tamping down the wefts. It never ceases to amaze that, with such basic apparatus, a woman is able to produce such skilfully woven and finely designed pieces of art.

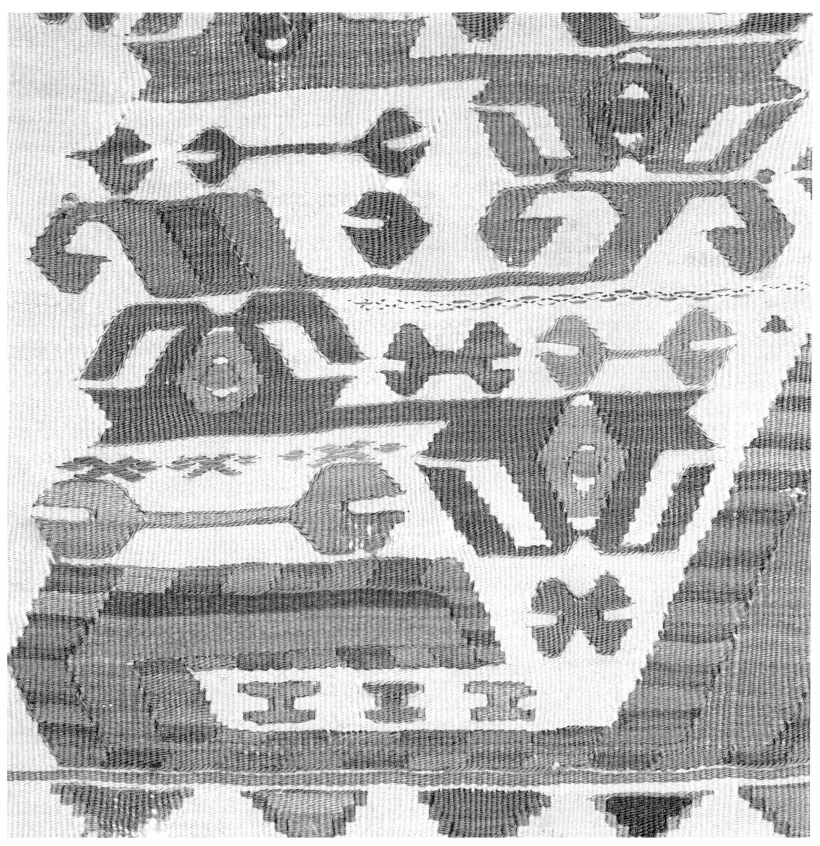

FIGURE 3: *The splendid use of harmonising colours in an Aydinli kilim – detail of plate 20.*

COLOURS AND DYEING

Until the discovery of synthetic dyes towards the end of last century, weavers obtained their colours from plants and other natural sources available to them. Certain dye substances became important items of trade – notably indigo, derived from a plant native to India and some other tropical countries.

Many of the processes to extract dyes from their raw materials were lengthy and complicated. Consequently, when cheap synthetic substitutes, with their great range of colours, appeared on the market, weavers in many areas readily turned to them. This often resulted in weavings being produced with a clashing amalgam of colour instead of the balanced harmony of the older pieces, the latter dictated by generations of experience using the natural substances.

These early synthetic products, usually described as aniline dyes, had some poor attributes. They were not fast – instead they tended to bleach and run. Many were acidic and consequently weakened the wool fibres, so that the rugs wore easily. Unfortunately, these detrimental features became noticeable only after several years. Meanwhile large numbers of weavings employing these poor colours had been produced.

A big improvement in quality came with the development of chrome dyes. They are easy to use, come in a great variety of shades, and do not possess the dubious qualities of the aniline ones. The best of them are, however, prohibitively expensive, quite out of the range of the village weaver.

Synthetic dyes steadily penetrated weaving areas, so that one could safely say that the majority of weavings produced over the last forty to sixty years contained them. Some nomadic people continued to obtain at least some of their colours from natural sources. This is to be expected where tribal people are isolated from trade routes and where, moreover, to purchase a full range of colours requires a considerable monetary outlay.

Let us dispel one myth at this point: plant colours are not necessarily soft and subdued. In fact good natural dyes can be fresh and vibrant and remain resistant to fading. As they are never chemically pure they usually mellow with age, producing harmonious variations in colour, whereas synthetic dyes tend to remain too uniform. We should not, however, denigrate synthetic dyes, for the best of them are more acceptable than poor natural ones.

The village dyer was a highly esteemed artisan. There was almost an aura of mystery surrounding his craft. Recipes for obtaining certain shades of colour were carefully guarded secrets, kept within the family and handed down from one generation to the next. Unfortunately, within the last hundred years or so, social changes and political upheavals, coupled with the advent of chemical dyes, saw the demise of natural dyeing.

Today, with the resurgence of interest in natural dyes in the Turkish weaving industry, some rug makers are struggling to obtain the glorious colours of the past. While their efforts are to be commended, some shades of colour seem beyond their reach. Chemical analysis of the old dyes can suggest what plant was used, but the actual dyeing process used to obtain certain hues is in some cases a long-lost secret.

The villager or nomad was not able to control the dyeing procedure as carefully as the town or city dyer, so tribal weavings typically possessed considerable variation in colour. Because they did not have the means to dye large batches of wool at a time, a succession of dye lots could result in quite large differences in shades of one colour. The degree of penetration of the dye was affected by the varying tightness of twist of the homespun wool. Also, wool to the outside of each hank took up the dye more quickly than that to the inside. Further gradations in hue also depended on the time of the year that the raw materials were gathered, since the quality of dye rendered from some plants differed quite markedly from season to season.

These variations in colour usually became apparent after some time and with the agency of light. They take the form of subtle nuances or bands of different shades, called abrash, which are typical of most older weavings where natural dyes have been used. Today, many rugs have abrash purposely woven in, but the effect is always too deliberate to look real.

Sometimes one finds kilims where whole areas appear to have undergone colour changes. It happens that one batch of a certain colour is not fixed properly and subsequently alters with time. Or it may simply be that the weaver ran out of one shade and completed the weaving with the wools she had left. In some areas blue and aubergine were commonly juxtaposed; whereas the two colours may have been originally fairly similar in intensity, the aubergine often faded to a lilac or soft grey, while the blue remained constant. Two-part kilims also often show considerable differences in colour – this is understandable when one considers that several months may have elapsed between the weaving of one half and the completion of the other.

Generally, before wool takes up the dye it must be mordanted so that the colour penetrates the fibres and becomes fixed. As most natural dyes are weak organic acids, salts of metals are suitable mordants. The wool is either first boiled in the mordant solution, or the mordant is added to the dye bath. Alum was the most commonly used mordant. It is found in many parts of Turkey and for centuries was an important item of export from that country. Of all mordants, it has the least effect on the hue of the dye. Alum-mordanted wool produces clear colours.

Iron sulphate, another common mordant, tends to darken colours. Tin chloride was used unintentionally, as it was a corrosion product from the copper vessels commonly used for dyeing, many of which were tinned. Its effect on colours is to brighten them. Copper sulphate, another widely used mordant, imparts bluish or greenish shades to the dye. More recently, chrome (potassium dichromate) has been available as a mordant, but it is not known to have been used in Turkey. It intensifies colours, at the same time providing a greenish cast.

Dyers recognised that colours extracted from bark or some roots did not require a mordant; in fact, the tannic acid in these materials acted as a direct mordant.

With the addition of various substances to the dye bath, different shades of colour could be obtained. Common additives used were tartar (cream of tartar, a by-product of wine making), citric acid, or wood ashes. Urine was reputedly added to modify certain colours. None of these substances is, strictly speaking, a mordant.

Submitting the wool to acidic or alkaline mordants, or boiling it for some time in dye baths, can have a deleterious result on its life. The degree of corrosion of the wool fibres in some old weavings shows the effect of the harsh treatment which was necessary to obtain certain colours.

Red, blue and yellow are the basic colours in rug weaving. Using these colours, together with a black, natural undyed brown and white wool, the weaver can obtain all the variations she requires.

Madder (*Rubia tinctorum*), a plant that grows wild in many parts of the Middle East, was the main source of red. It used to be specifically cultivated for dye production. From its fleshy roots a wide range of colours may be obtained, from pink, through to dark red, scarlet and aubergine, as well as orange. Madder contains up to nine different dye compounds; the final colour of the dye depends on the age of the root, the method of extraction of the dye, the temperature of the dye bath, the mordant used and whether any additives were included in the dye.

The process of dye extraction from madder is not simple. Usually two- or three-year-old roots are selected, dried and ground up. The crushed root material is soaked in water for two days and then simmered for about half an hour, until the dye is released. The dye bath is left standing for another day, then reheated and the mordanted wool added – for a given weight of wool about an equal amount of madder root is required. The dye bath is immediately removed from the heat and the wool left to soak in the dye bath for a further two or three days. With alum mordanted wool, the result is an orange-red; with the addition of cream of tartar or citric acid a bright red is obtained. If iron salts are added instead, the wool dyes to an aubergine colour.

There are many references to kermes red, a crimson dye obtained from the gall-like female scale insects which infest a Mediterranean oak. Although some authorities refute its use as a dye for rugs, the extract from these insects has been known since antiquity and was an export from Macedonia and Mediterranean Turkish areas until it was replaced by the American cochineal. Our word "crimson" is actually derived from the Arabic term for the kermes insect.

During the course of last century, cochineal red began to be used in the weavings of some areas. Extracted from the cochineal scale insect

(*Dactylopius coccus costa*), a parasite of the prickly pear cactus, it was first introduced into the Middle East from its native countries, Mexico and Guatemala, via Spain. Cultivation of this insect commenced in Spain and the Canary Islands in the early part of the 19th century, and the production of cochineal soon assumed considerable importance. For example, by 1869, 2.7 million kilograms of cochineal was exported. Only the female insects are used to extract the dye. To obtain 1 kilogram of dye about 150 000 insects have to be gathered.[*]

The dye substance in the cochineal scale insect is carmine red, which yields a bluish red colour. With the addition of cream of tartar, alum mordanted wool becomes bright red; by adding iron sulphate to the dye bath a purplish colour is produced.

Indigo, extracted from the Indian plant *Indigofera tinctoria*, has long been regarded as the traditional source of blue dye. However, the indigo contained in the oldest Turkish weavings was probably obtained from locally grown woad (*Isatis tinctoria*), a plant which is also found in parts of Europe. This plant used to be widely cultivated in Turkey, but with the opening of trade routes and the consequent easier access to indigo from the East, cultivation of woad was gradually abandoned.

Extraction of the dye from either plant is laborious and complicated, taking two weeks or more to complete. First the plant material is fermented in water; honey or sugar may be added to speed up the bacterial action. Urine was usually added to act as a reducing agent to render the insoluble dye compounds soluble. Finally, the dye bath is made alkaline with the addition of slaked lime and then the wool immersed. During the whole process, care must be taken not to unduly disturb the surface of the liquid.

The blue colour does not become apparent until the wool is exposed to the air, when oxidation of the dye occurs. The dyer may have to return the wool to the dye bath several times until the desired shade of blue is obtained.

Indigo blue is a surface dye which merely lies on the outside of the wool fibres. Hence it is not resistant to abrasion. The blue areas of many old kilims show a rubbed look, where the white of the original wool shows through.

In the 18th century the sulphonate of indigo was developed by treating indigo with sulphuric acid. Unlike indigo, it is water soluble and it dyes alum mordanted, or unmordanted, wool a fast deep blue.

A carpet dealer we know in Istanbul, who wanted to make up some indigo-dyed wool for his repairmen, explained how, in his village in the east of Turkey, the vat of fermenting indigo material was packed around with donkey dung. The heat of the decomposing dung provided the right temperature for the fermentation process. He lamented the fact that donkey dung and urine – the latter to be added to the dye bath – was difficult to obtain in Istanbul, but decided anyway to try to produce

---

[*] Figures obtained from the Turkish and Islamic Museum, Ibrahim Paşa, Istanbul.

the colour. For two weeks he subjected his neighbouring dealers to the putrid smell of the decaying matter and had to suffer many taunts and curses for his troubles.

He showed the results he obtained – a dull greyish blue. "If only I could get donkey dung!" he complained.

There are many plants growing in Turkey that were used for yellow. Weld (*Reseda luteola*) yields a brilliant, fast yellow on alum mordanted wool, as does the fruit of buckthorn (*Rhamnus petiolaris*). The heart-wood of dyer's sumac (*Cotinis coggrygia*) – known to gardeners as the smoke bush – gives a clear yellow which gradually becomes duller and browner on exposure to light. It is seen in the weavings from around Fethiye, West Turkey, and also from Erzerum-Kars in the north-east.

The flowers of white chamomile (*Anthemis chia*) and some of the widespread and common spurges (*Euphorbia* spp.) also produce clear, fast yellows. The fresh dried leaves and shoots of *Rhus coriaria* yield a yellow with alum mordanted wool, but on iron mordanted wool the result is black. Most of these dyes have been used since ancient times for dyeing textiles.

Sage, quince, gooseberry, grapevine leaves, pomegranate peelings, thyme, barberry, mullein, sorrel and some species of *Hypericum* (St John's wort) have all been used in the past to obtain yellow. With each of these dyes, by altering the mordant and additives, colours ranging from pale yellow, or straw, to tobacco can be attained.

Saffron, a dye gained from the stigmas of crocus flowers, provided a very pure and bright yellow. However, to obtain sufficient dye material was intensely laborious and therefore it was rarely used.

Although the weavers of the past were able to obtain shades of green directly from plant sources, the green with the most attractive appearance and the most character was made by overdyeing yellow-dyed wool with indigo. Sometimes one of the colours is transient, so in time the green tends to blue or else to yellow.

For brown areas of a weaving, wool of a natural brown colour is sometimes used, but it is more usual to find that the wool has been dyed to obtain the desired colour. Some of the yellow-yielding dye plants can be made to produce shades from beige to mustard by varying the mordant or additives. One of the most common sources of brown is walnut husks. Being a direct dye, it acts on unmordanted wool to produce shades from a yellow-brown to a dark brown.

Black was usually obtained from the fruit cups of various oaks, particularly the Vallonia oak (*Quercus makrolepis*). Oak-apples, the fruit-like growths on leaves, induced by the presence of the larvae of small gall wasps which feed on the leaves, were also commonly used. These dye substances contain considerable amounts of tannic acid, which in combination with an iron mordant produces various shades from dark brown to black. Unfortunately this dyeing process has a corrosive effect on the wool. In older weavings the wool in the black-dyed areas is often very brittle and tends to wear away quickly. Weavers must have been aware of this effect, for the motifs of piled rugs are often outlined in black – as the rug ages and the black wears down, the other colours stand out in relief. Producers of modern rugs often have the black edging trimmed down to simulate this aging process.

Many of the magnificent, strong natural colours we see in older kilims may never be recreated. As we suggested earlier, synthetic dyes are generally easier to use. Moreover, whereas the villager may have been able to produce up to thirty shades of colour from natural sources, chemical dyes can provide a couple of thousand or more.

So what of the future? Will tomorrow's collectors have to be satisfied with purely commercial items made from machine-spun yarns which are chemically dyed? With the rapidly changing lifestyles and increasing cost of labour in those Middle East countries where weavings have been traditionally made, it may well seem that the old craft is in its death throes.

There is a growing interest in returning to the use of natural dyes and hand-spun materials. While the splendid works of art, reflecting generations of tribal culture, may never be woven again – and copies of these pieces can never stand up to the real thing – it is pleasant to see that some effort is being put into trying to recapture the charm of natural dyes. Still, as all these ventures have been established with purely commercial gain in mind, one wonders whether, ultimately, the weavers will have the time and the patience to carry out the laborious processes of dye extraction such as they were in the past.

The majority of kilims being woven today use synthetic dyes. Many have such harsh, unsympathetic colours that there is a growing industry in sunning them to tone them down. We know of agents who collect these outlandish objects by the truckload from the warehouses of Istanbul and take them to villages surrounding Malatya or Konya, where several weeks of sunning make their colours more acceptable. On a visit to a remote village in the Taurus Mountains one of the authors saw several hundred of these "sunshine" kilims, as the dealers so aptly call them, spread out in the dust of the village square. People were trampling across them, hens scratched among them, while young lambs and kids gambolled about and even urinated on them. Garishly coloured new kilims were rapidly being transposed into "antiques", complete with a variety of stains.

TECHNIQUES

TAPESTRY WEAVES: These are the true kilims, although the word kilim is often commonly applied to other types of flatweaves. Basically, this is a plain weave technique, where the wefts are passed over and under each of the warps. The designs are formed by discontinuous wefts of different colours being woven back and forth in the design areas, instead of being carried right across the weaving, as in ordinary cloth weaves. Owing to the nature of this technique, slits are normally left at the vertical boundaries between adjacent colours, where each weft turns round the warp at the edge of the design area; hence most kilims are slit-tapestry weaves.

The shape of the motifs is governed by the very nature of this type of weaving. Naturally, the weaver tries to avoid long slits, as they would tend to weaken the textile excessively. Thus rectangular designs often have stepped edges (fig. 4). The smaller the steps, the tighter the weave. Otherwise the motifs are designed so that the boundaries are diagonal or curvilinear (fig. 5), the latter created by weaving in the weft eccentrically. Some kilims incorporate all of these methods.

Dovetailing (also called interlocking or warp sharing), where wefts of adjoining colours turn around the same warp along their common vertical boundary, so avoiding slits, is rarely found in Turkish kilims. It is a technique, however, that is quite widely used in Iran and is also common to weavings of Central America. The motifs are never so clear-cut and precise as those using the slit-tapestry method.

Typical of many Turkish kilims is the outlining of the figures by one or more threads of a different colour. The insertion of these extra wefts is done while the designs are being created, not afterwards as many might suppose. In a technique referred to as eccentric weft outlining, two or more wefts of a contrasting colour are woven with an ordinary, over one warp under the next method between adjacent colours. These extra wefts lie obliquely to the main lie of the weave as they follow the contours of the

FIGURE 4: Stepped edges, typical of Karakeçili kilims – detail of plate 12.

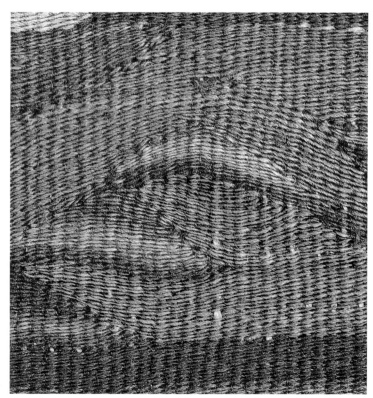

FIGURE 5: Eccentric wefting in a Şarköy kilim – detail of plate 1.

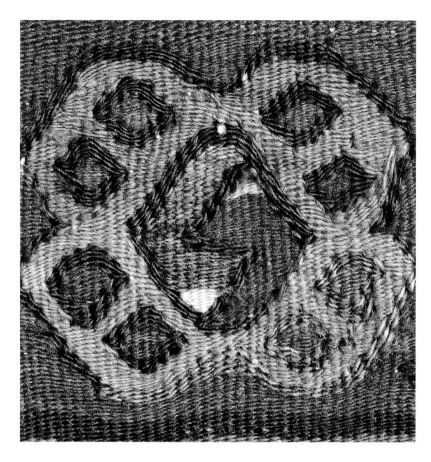

FIGURE 6: Eccentric weft outlining.

FIGURE 7: Contour weft wrapping.

motifs (fig. 6). Another method, contour weft wrapping, entails passing an extra weft progressively across two warps and back under one, soumak style, along the boundary of a design (fig. 7). The outlining weft is raised slightly above the surface of the fabric and thus is usually the first to suffer abrasion and wear.

Both methods delineate the designs with more emphasis and also help to strengthen their boundaries.

The slit-tapestry technique is used for pieces ranging from small bags and cushions, and prayer kilims, up to large pieces several square metres in size.

SOUMAK: This is a weft-wrapping technique where the design threads are carried progressively across usually two warps, back under one, in a continuous process until the edge of the design is reached. Using the same method, the weaver then returns the weft in the opposite direction. A herringbone effect is often created owing to the nature of the opposing slopes of the weft loops of each row as they cross the warps.

Although an over two, back under one sequence of weft insertion is the most common, one can find soumaks with 3:1 or 4:2 ratios.

The soumak weaves most frequently found are brocades – that is, after each row of design wefts one or more ground wefts are inserted with a normal over one, under one method (see fig. 8). The ground wefts are generally much finer than the design wefts and are often difficult to see in the finished weaving. In Turkey, this technique was mainly used for the manufacture of sturdy storage bags or cushions, many splendid examples of which can still be found (see plates 32 and 49). Large soumak brocade rugs mostly originate from the Caucasus and Azerbaijan.

In pure soumaks there are no ground wefts. Consequently slits occur between vertical boundaries of adjacent colours. The motifs are often contour weft wrapped with a thread of contrasting colour to make them stand out. Pure soumak weaves are not very common. Most are finely worked and delicate, and although they are often woven in the form of bags, they were probably respected and treated gently. Today, however, one sometimes sees beautiful old pieces which have been severely damaged because they have been used to store grain. As holes appeared the owners merely patched them up with pieces of cloth, or crocheted the holes together with a spider web of often brightly coloured threads.

Rarer still is a type of soumak weave in which instead of weaving the design wefts in both directions, the weaver carries them straight back across the reverse side of the textile after completing each row, so that the face of the weave shows wefts worked in one direction only. This results in a weaving with a double thickness of wefts, creating an embossed effect. Again, this technique is usually used to make bags. Thin lustrous yarn is almost invariably used in their manufacture, allowing the designs to be worked in fine detail (see fig. 9).

The word "soumak" is said to be derived from Shemakha, a town in the eastern Caucasus. This has led to some confusion in the past because virtually all soumak weaves were ascribed to the Caucasus. In fact, this technique was used by diverse people in Turkey and Iran as well, and also by the Turkomans and Belouchis.

Some books erroneously describe soumak brocade as a needle stitch because of its similarity in its completed effect to stem-stitch embroidery. Even today some otherwise knowledgeable dealers make this mistake.

If we accept that brocading is the insertion during the weaving process of design wefts supplementary to the ground weave, this distinguishes it from embroidery, where the designs are stitched onto a ready-made canvas. The design wefts of brocades pass, or "float", over and under varying numbers of warps, depending on the technique; they are sometimes worked back and forth in the design area, and sometimes carried right across the weaving.

The most common types of weft-float brocades are cicim (pronounced "jijim") and zili. Soumak brocades, already described, where the wefts actually wrap the warps as they are inserted, form a separate category.

CICIM:
This technique is used to produce scattered or crowded motifs against usually a balanced ground weave (fig. 10). On the whole,

FIGURE 8: Soumak brocade of the common countered type.

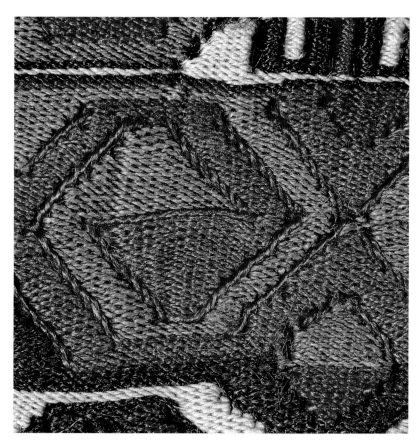

FIGURE 9: Pure soumak worked in one direction – detail of plate 81.

the motifs are narrow and angular. The weaver works from the back of the fabric; taking each of the various-coloured design wefts in turn, she passes it to the front of the weaving, floats it across three or four warps, and then returns it towards her and leaves it hanging, before picking up the next thread and inserting it in the same manner. After she has worked right across the weaving, introducing the coloured threads according to the design, she adds ground wefts, usually of the same colour and thickness as the warps, and beats them down.

With the next row, the weaver carries the design wefts back under the warps to the leading edge of her motifs before they are passed to the front of the weaving again. In effect, on their return the design wefts wrap around the warps in the design areas. The reverse side of the cicim often looks untidy because of the loose ends of the coloured threads which are left hanging. Even with crowded designs, areas of ground weave remain visible in the finished weaving.

We have observed that, when making larger cicims, often two women work from the back

FIGURE 10: Cicim brocade.

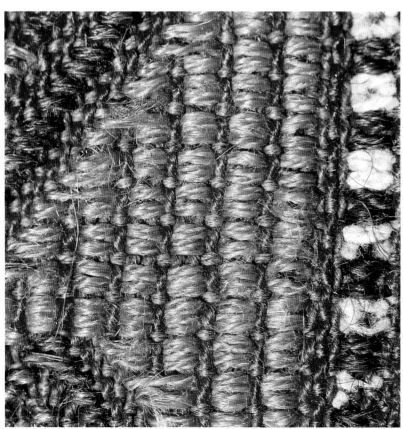

FIGURE 11: Zili brocade with weft floats carried over three warps, under one.

FIGURE 12: Offset zili brocade with wefts carried over three warps, under three – detail of plate 87.

while a third works from the front; the task of the last is to control the regularity of the designs and to beat down the wefts.

The cicim technique is used to make large rugs, decorative covers, bags, cushions, and so on.

ZILI: The zili technique was widely used in Turkey for the manufacture of finely designed bags, cushions and larger pieces. A favourite zili wall-hanging often took pride of place in many village homes.

In the basic zili method, supplementary design wefts are floated progressively forward over and under warps, usually in a 3:1 ratio (see figs 11 and 12), although variations such as 3:3 and 5:1 are also common. After each row of design wefts, one or more shoots of ground weft are woven in and beaten down. At the edges of each motif the coloured wefts are drawn vertically across the ground wefts before being woven in the reverse direction. This feature helps to distinguish zilis from cicims, so an examination of the reverse side of the weaving is often essential. Where the design completely fills the weaving, the face of the fabric often has a corded appearance, created by certain of the warps being left uncovered over long distances by the weft floats.

Many of the scattered brocade motifs that decorate kilims are woven in using a zili technique. These motifs are sometimes an integral part of the total design and, as such, are important additions (see plate 40).

One of the most common techniques employed in weaving bags is often mistakenly referred to as offset reverse soumak. Allied to zili, this method is used to obtain strong diagonal designs – it is in fact a series of over two under two weft floats, not soumak at all, where, as we have explained, the wefts are wrapped around warps. To obtain the angular patterns, the design wefts are offset at the edge of the colour zones by passing them under either one warp, or more usually three, before they are returned in the opposite direction. This can be seen by examining the underside of the weaving. The design wefts are usually worked in both directions before the ground wefts are laid down (see fig. 13).

There is also a technique for which no name

FIGURE 13: Modified zili brocade with floats carried over two warps, under two – detail of plate 89.

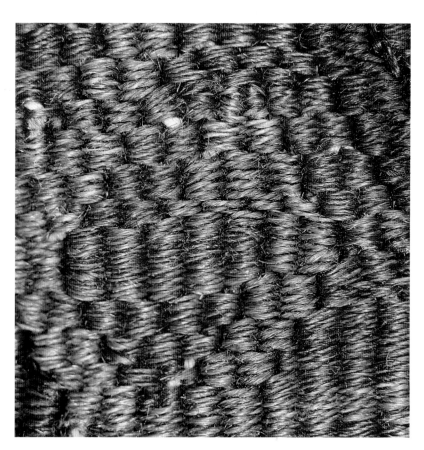

FIGURE 14: Detail of technique using weft floats carried over two warps, under two. In this method ground wefts are omitted.

FIGURE 15: *This technique lends itself to motifs with a diagonal design. Note the weft-wrapping around the motifs.*

seems to exist. Likewise found mainly in the form of small bags, from the Malatya-Maraş area of Turkey, this method involves design wefts being passed over and under pairs of warps four or five times in succession before being offset by one warp and the process repeated. The result is designs made up of little blocks of colour with a diagonal arrangement (fig. 14). Although not a brocade, since ground wefts are not added, we have included it here because of its obvious relationship to the last technique described.

WARP-FACED TEXTILES:

All methods described up to now are weft-faced – that is, the wefts are packed down over the warps to form the visible surface of the weaving. There are, however, many examples of warp-faced textiles available, where it is from different-coloured warps that the motifs are created. In this method the warps are arranged in alternating bands of different colours on the loom, according to the design that is going to be made. Warps of the desired colour are picked up by ground wefts to create a motif of one colour against the background of another.

This method of weaving lends itself to the creation of long, narrow strips. Tent bands, saddle and bag straps and ornamental animal trappings are made this way (see fig. 16). The strips can be cut and joined to make wider pieces for saddlecloths and other decorative covers.

Sometimes one finds carefully executed two-faced fabrics made with this method of weaving. In these, a design in one colour on one side is in the complementary colour on the reverse. Some of the most intricately designed examples we have seen are old pieces woven of fine alpaca hair by the Indians of Peru and Bolivia.

Strangely, in the Turkish rug trade, warp-faced fabrics are occasionally referred to as cicims, although their method of manufacture and appearance are so obviously different. This confusion is perhaps brought about by the similar-sounding word "jajim", used by the Iranians to describe pieces woven with this technique.

FIGURE 16: *Warp-faced weaving in a çuval strap – detail of plate 39.*

PART TWO

PLATE 1

ŞARKÖY KILIM

Size: 146 x 108 cm.

Warp: Wool, S plied   41/10 cm.

Weft: Wool, Z spun   280/10 cm.

Colours: Seven – red, dark blue, light blue, blue-green, light brown, pale grey, dark grey.

Technique: Eccentric weft tapestry.

Condition: Good – it has small amounts of repair to one end.

With their unusual design and colours, Şarköy and Manastir kilims represent an anomalous group when compared with the bulk of Turkish flatweaves. Although many Turkish dealers swear that these kilims all originate from Thrace, the European section of Turkey, the question of their provenance is more obscure. There is a village called Şarköy located at the entrance of the Dardanelles. The name Manastir is even more enigmatic because it means monastery in Turkish. Seemingly neither name has any relevance to the origins of these kilims. Suffice to say both are terms so firmly entrenched in the language of rug enthusiasts that they continue to be used.

As the Ottoman Empire was extended into Europe the sultans endeavoured to firmly establish their hold over the conquered territory by settling groups of Turkic nomads there. This policy was also used to weaken powerful tribal unions within the Turkish mainland. Tribes which might otherwise have proved troublesome to their Ottoman rulers were forcibly resettled away from their sphere of power. The supplanted tribes continued their weaving practices but they were now divorced from the steadying influences of their age-old cultures, welded as they were to their native lands. They came into contact with designs and colours used by local people. From this intermingling of the different groups new forms arose.

Şarköy kilims were probably woven in the Bulgarian and Yugoslavian sectors of the Ottoman Empire. There is definitely a relationship in design and colour between them and the more recognisably Yugoslavian kilims.

PLATE 2

MANASTIR PRAYER KILIM

Size: 200 x 129 cm.

Warp: Wool, dark brown S plied   41/10 cm.

Weft: Wool, Z spun   220/10 cm.

Colours: Seven – blue, wine red, cochineal red, yellow, pale yellow, dark brown, white.

Technique: Slit-tapestry with some contour weft wrapping.

Condition: Good – the ends have been restored.

When the Ottoman Empire broke up after World War I, a large number of the Turkish settlers returned to Anatolia, bringing with them their weavings. Many of the émigrés settled in the west of Turkey, some around Konya. Here, those who continued weaving were subjected to new influences and had to adjust to the local colours and materials. So we can find more recent kilims, obviously Manastir in design, but more crudely woven than the older pieces emanating from the Balkans, and employing a different range of colours.

The so-called Manastir kilims are probably the product of Turkic people settled in Bulgaria, Romania and perhaps the northern part of Greece. The line separating Manastir and Şarköy kilims is at times very indistinct. Both types are single-piece kilims, often squarer in format than most other Turkish kilims and sometimes quite large. The designation Şarköy is given to those kilims with repetitive floral or geometric designs, woven using finely spun wool in deep blues, reds and greens, and with extensive use of eccentric wefting. Animal forms, often birdlike, are sometimes included. A distinctive subgroup consists mainly of larger pieces with geometric designs, where pale reddish brown and yellow predominate, and pale blues are used. The piece in plate 1 is rather unusual because of its smaller size.

Manastir kilims, on the other hand, generally have a simple pattern and a more open field. The palette of colours is also somewhat different – brighter reds and blues, and mustard yellow. Fine cotton was used for the warps of some pieces from Bulgaria.

PLATE 3

BERGAMA ÇUVAL

Size: 110 x 65 cm.

Warp: Soft white wool, S plied   59/10 cm.

Weft: Wool, S plied for design areas, Z spun for the plain weave areas   180/10 cm.

Colours: Eleven – two shades of red, two shades of blue, turquoise, dark olive green, burnt orange, dark olive brown, yellow, maroon, ivory.

Technique: Bands of modified zili brocade (offset 2:2 floats) mixed with 2:1 soumak, separated by stripes of plain weave. Extra brocade motifs are added at the top and bottom of the çuval, as well as on the back, which consists of narrow stripes of plain weave in different colours.

Condition: Fairly good.

Special Notes: The çuval still has its original straps.

North-western Turkey consists largely of plains and valleys locked between rugged hills and low mountains. To the west the alpine slopes spill down to merge with a narrow coastal strip bordering the Aegean Sea. This is the land of Troy, made famous to us through Homer's *Iliad*, and of ancient Pergamum, now called Bergama, which once rivalled Alexandria as a centre of learning.

The Turkic tribes who made this region their homeland seemed to have retained a strong cultural affinity with their native Turkestan, for strangely, although this part of Anatolia is the closest to Europe, it is here that we find weavings with strong Turkoman motifs, worked in glowing reds and blues. They bear a striking resemblance to those found east of the Caspian Sea.

Over the centuries several Turkic groups migrated to this region. Although the people are settled today, until relatively recently nomadism was an essential way of life for many. Each group maintained its own cultural identity. Even as they became settled, often forcibly by decree of Ottoman sultans, the various tribal groups tended to establish separate villages, keeping their individual traditions and customs. Elders were democratically chosen under tribal law. If one proved incompetent he would be deposed and another person elected to his position. The elders were responsible for making important decisions, supervising the division of grazing grounds and water rights, dispensing justice, and so on.

Voluntary and enforced settlement of nomadic groups continued throughout the Ottoman period, so by the end of last century few true nomads remained in the area. Seminomadism, where the people moved with their flocks, camels and tents to the mountain pastures in the spring, returning to their villages in the autumn, persisted for some time. Even as the people became settled, they insisted they were Yörük – Turkmen nomads. As long as the tribal structure was retained those tribes with a strong weaving tradition continued to make their beautiful weavings.

The region, centred around Balikesir and Bergama, was – and is – renowned for the quality of its wool. Fine and glossy, it was used by highly skilled weavers to make some of the most splendid weavings known to collectors. Not least of these are their çuvals, among the finest and most beautiful textiles of Turkey (see plate 8). These pieces can best be appreciated by examining them closely, when the intricacy of their weave and subtle nuances of their colours are revealed. Common to many is the inclusion of two shades of red and two of blue used in close proximity to each other. Plate 4b illustrates this feature.

Plates 4a, b and c show details from three separate çuvals. The precisely drawn, vigorous figures are obtained using few colours. All are woven with the same technique, a form of zili brocade with over two under two floats, offset to achieve the diagonal shapes (see also fig. 13 in the section on techniques). A careful examination of plate 4c reveals the red ground wefts appearing in places between the rows of brocade wefts.

PLATE 4A

Plate 4B

PLATE 5

YAĞCEBEDIR ÇUVAL

Size: 107 x 71 cm.

Warp: Black goat hair, S plied   75/10 cm.

Weft: Ground weft of black goat hair, S plied
80/10 cm; design wefts wool, S plied.

Colours: Five – blue, red, orange, white, black (ground
weave).

Technique: Contour zili on a balanced weave; horizontal
lines are of soumak weft-wrapping.

Condition: Good, except for one small hole.

Of the tribal groups that came to occupy these
parts, the Yağcebedir are justifiably famous for
their weaving abilities. Now forcibly settled in
villages east of Bergama, such as Sindirği, the
women have continued to weave a variety of
textiles. The çuval in plate 5 was probably made
by a weaver of the Yağcebedir group. Using
only a few colours against a balanced weave of
finely spun black goat hair, she has created this
highly decorative piece. One has to admire her
skill involved in spinning the goat-hair foundation. To produce such a fine thread from such
robust and springy material is extraordinarily
difficult.

PLATE 6

YÜNCÜ YÖRÜK KILIM

Size: 230 x 125 cm.

Warp: Wool, S plied 36/10 cm.

Weft: Wool, Z spun and cotton (white areas)
240-260/10 cm.

Colours: Six – rust red, brown-red, dark blue, light blue,
ivory, white (cotton).

Technique: Slit-tapestry with contour weft wrapping;
narrow brocaded bands separate the main panels of
design; a few scattered brocade motifs are found on the
field.

Condition: The sides have been repaired but the
remainder of the kilim is in good condition.

The Yüncü Yörük tribe (Yüncü means wool
producer), now settled in villages in Balikesir
Province, produced weavings in which the predominant reds and blues were characteristically
relieved by small amounts of white, as can be
seen in the accompanying plate. Their designs
retain a very strong Turkoman influence.
Strangely, the same usage of colour can often
be found in some weavings produced by Kurdish groups from the region of Siirt in south-east
Turkey (see plate 90).

PLATE 7

YÜNCÜ YÖRÜK KILIM

Two-Piece; Detail

Size: 209 x 204 cm.

Warp: Wool, S plied   46/10 cm.

Weft: Wool, Z spun   140-280/10 cm; in a few areas two strands are inserted together.

Colours: Eight – madder red (variable), pale red, dark blue, greenish blue, green (used in one small area only), straw yellow, orange, white.

Technique: Slit-tapestry weave; some contour weft wrapping still persists; scattered weft float brocade motifs.

Condition: It has had some repair.

Seen at first hand this kilim is very striking, but reduced to the format of a page the design loses its impressiveness. It is for this reason that only about one-quarter is shown here.

As in the kilim shown previously, the reds and blues immediately catch the eye; only gradually does one begin to appreciate the other shades, which are subtly used. This kilim was made by a skilled weaver. It has a wonderful textural aspect brought about both by variations in thickness of the wefts and the way they are applied quite eccentrically in some places.

In the past a few Yüncü Yörük kilims, usually distinguishable through their columnar latch-hook designs and prevailing red and blue colouration, found their way into the market-place. Today, it is very rare indeed to see them for sale in the bazaars of Istanbul or elsewhere.

PLATE 8

YÜNCÜ YÖRÜK ÇUVAL

Size: 88 x 69 cm.

Warp: Wool, S plied   56/10 cm.

Weft: Wool, Z spun in plain weave areas
220/10 cm; S plied in design areas.

Colours: Nine – blue, dark blue, red, orange-red,
touches of ivory, white (cotton), gold metallic thread,
pale yellow and pale green silk.

Technique: The design bands are worked in modified zili
(mainly offset 2:2 floats) separated by bands of plain
weft-faced weave.

Condition: Good.

This çuval sums up most of the features that
make this area of weaving so distinctive and, at
the same time, so appealing. The shifts in colour
are subtle, with the preponderance of red and
blue being relieved here and there by touches
of silk and metallic thread. The use of white
cotton is confined to mere specks in the centre
of the double hominoid figures of one major
band of design and to the petals of some of the
half rosettes in the other. Using her restricted
palette (which is, however, dyed over superior
wool), the weaver has gone to considerable
lengths to vary the pattern throughout the çuval.

PLATE 9
BERGAMA COVER

Size: 241 x 156 cm.

Warp: Wool, S plied   52/10 cm.

Weft: Wool, Z spun, ground weave   150/10 cm.

Colours: Ten – two blues, red, brick red, maroon-red, turquoise, orange, lilac, dark brown, white.

Technique: Mainly chequered 3:3 zili, plus contour zili. Warp ends are plaited into tassels and bound with coloured wool.

Condition: Very good.

Zili brocade rugs of the type shown here are frequently called Verneh in the trade, an appellation that has led to some unfortunate confusion, since the name Verneh is apparently Caucasian and is more correctly applied to some brocade rugs from these parts. Thus, pieces like this one were often, in the past, ascribed to the Caucasus instead of the Bergama region of Turkey. The quality of the wool and colours is very typical of this region, and many similarities can be found in çuvals woven here.

PLATE 10

BALIKESIR COVER

Size: 214 x 158 cm.

Warp: Wool, S plied   52/10 cm.

Weft: Wool, Z spun   160-260/10 cm.

Colours: Five – madder red, blue, white, yellow, black.

Technique: Slit-tapestry weave.

Condition: Reasonable – it has had some wear.

Striking in its simplicity, its wonderful matured colours and the texture of its weave, this kilim has great appeal. The varying thicknesses of the wefts and the way they are inserted eccentrically in many areas makes the rich madder-red field far from static. The yellow used is especially strong, its intensity emphasised by being placed alongside the black.

Old, plain field kilims of this sort are uncommon. Known as sofra, these weavings are generally considered to have been used for placing the food on at meal times. Traditionally in Turkey, particularly in the rural areas, tables are not used. Instead, the food is served in a large, communal dish set on a low stand, around which the diners sit cross-legged on the floor, helping themselves.

PLATE 11

KARAKEÇILI KILIM

Size: 267 x 170 cm.

Warp: Wool, S plied   44/10 cm.

Weft: Wool, Z spun   110-170/10 cm.

Colours: Thirteen – dark blue, light blue, light greenish blue, dark greenish blue, red, vermilion, two oranges, brownish red, maroon, pale yellow, dark brown, white.

Technique: Slit-tapestry with many scattered zili brocade figures. The end with the warp loops has the remains of a chain of black goat hair running through it; at the other end the warps have been braided to form a thick band and then bundles of them plaited into tassels. A strip of two-colour zili, giving the impression of twining, finishes off this end.

Condition: Good.

Kilims attributed to the Karakeçili are found mostly in the west of Turkey, especially from the Balikesir-Kütahya area. However, this once-powerful tribe used to have a very extensive range – various groups of Karakeçili were found almost as far east as Lake Van, northwards in the Ankara and Eskişehir areas, and in the south towards Adana. During World War I a contingent of Karakeçili tribesmen formed part of the 4th Division of the Kurdish irregular cavalry, recruited from around Viranşehir, a town near Urfa in south-east Turkey. The Karakeçilis fought valiantly alongside the Kurds on the Turkish front against the Russians. The Karakeçilis (meaning the "black goat" people) were one of the original tribes to invade Asia Minor. They have retained their tribal name, unlike many subgroups in Anatolia which later assumed tribal status and adopted a clan name, leading to such present-day confusion over affinities between different groups.

Plate 11 shows a Karakeçili kilim from the Kütahya-Balikesir area. One's eye is immediately drawn to the large, white, hooked motifs, before taking in the fact that they in turn enclose complex hooked designs which contain inside them other, smaller ones. The intricacies of the total design become more obvious when one becomes aware of the rocket-like motifs with reciprocating hooks that occupy the spaces along the sides of the kilim, between the barbs of the white figures.

Although it is not finely woven, this kilim's bold designs, plus the varied use of colour, make it an interesting piece.

PLATE 12

KARAKEÇILI KILIM
Two-Piece

Size: 306 x 156 cm.

Warp: Wool, S plied   49/10 cm.

Weft: Wool, Z spun   220-300/10 cm.

Colours: Sixteen – blue, light blue, greenish blue, grey, olive green, pale green, bright red, deep madder red, brick red, cochineal red, orange, yellow, maroon, deep aubergine, brown, ivory.

Technique: Slit-tapestry with contour weft wrapping around small motifs, plus extra brocade figures.

Condition: Good – the sides have been restored.

There are certain features that characterise Karakeçili kilims. These include a predominant use of deep blues and reds, a field commonly comprising a series of bold multihooked designs, and end borders featuring starlike motifs. The most typical characteristic is the stepped edges of the designs (see fig. 4).

Although featuring design properties distinctive of Karakeçili, the piece shown appears from its colours to have been woven further to the south-west than the preceding kilim. It could be mistaken for an Aydinli kilim, especially with the latch-hook side borders which are so commonly used in Aydinli weavings. Nevertheless, the border was also known to Karakeçili weavers, as well as to tribal groups around Sivrihisar. Altogether a much finer and more skilfully woven kilim than that shown in plate 11, this is of a considerably older generation. The drawing is very precise, and the numerous colours, which are dyed over lustrous wool, are employed with both a certitude and a tremendous sense of harmony, all suggesting the work of a very experienced weaver. Even though a two-piece kilim, unlike plate 11, the basic design is the same, but with a shift in emphasis. The figures along the sides are particularly eye-catching. It is a piece that can be greatly appreciated in its entirety or by concentrating on small areas of it at a time.

PLATE 13

KELES KILIM

Size: 183 x 133 cm.

Warp: Wool, S plied   45/10 cm.

Weft: Wool, Z spun   160-200/10 cm.

Colours: Nine – blue, dark blue, turquoise, green, two reds, orange, dark brown, white.

Technique: Bands of slit-tapestry and plain weave; contour weft wrapping around some motifs.

Condition: Good – it has had some repair.

With such an obviously different concept in design compared with any of the other pieces already shown from the north-western part of Turkey, it might, at first, seem hard to justify placing this kilim in this section. However, the quality of its wool, its weave and its colours are all very typical of the Bergama-Balikesir region. As one examines it more closely, one becomes aware of the minor borders on either side of the main panels of design, also found in some of the çuvals produced here. An old piece, this kilim is attributed to weavers from the region of Keles, a small village in the mountains south of Bursa.

PLATE 14

AYDINLI KILIM
Two-Piece

Size: 280 x 155 cm.

Warp: Wool, S plied   40/10 cm.

Weft: Wool, Z spun   280/10 cm.

Colours: Ten – blue, red, maroon-red, orange, yellow, purplish mauve, olive grey, pale lilac, brown, white.

Technique: Slit-tapestry with eccentric weft outlining around some motifs, plus additional brocade figures.

Condition: Good – it has had some restoration.

The white ground kilims of the Aydinli are quite distinctive. They are strongly tribal in design, the larger pieces usually being woven in two parts, and sometimes in three. Ramshorn hooks feature prominently; they are developed into large heraldic figures occupying the centre field of the kilims, or as repetitive, reciprocal designs worked mostly in red and dark brown along the outer borders. The end borders also frequently consist of reciprocal figures. Stylised, double-headed, animal-like motifs can be found in the field of some older pieces (plates 18 and 20); they have been somewhat modified here.

PLATE 15

AYDINLI KILIM
Two-Piece

Size: 247 x 150 cm.

Warp: Wool, S plied   42/10 cm.

Weft: Wool, Z spun   220/10 cm.

Colours: Ten – red, coral red, pinkish red, blue, yellow, green, blue-green, mauve, dark brown, white; some metallic thread.

Technique: Slit-tapestry with eccentric weft outlining around some motifs, plus additional brocade figures.

Condition: Good.

Aydin, east of Ephesus, is a bustling town in western Turkey. It is a centre for agricultural produce and renowned for the quality of its figs. Named after the Aydinli tribe, it is not, as many dealers would have one believe, the place where all so-called Aydin kilims were woven.

The Aydinli tribal group was once a powerful confederation in western Turkey. For diverse reasons, including the policy of various sultans of splitting up such strong groups, segments of the tribe were relocated in different parts of Anatolia. Consequently, Aydinli kilims can be found which were woven in places as far apart as Kütahya and Adana regions, each subgroup being subjected to the varying influences of the different environments. The piece shown here, judging from its range of colours and some of its minor design elements, appears to have come from the northern limits of the tribal range, from the area around Sivrihisar.

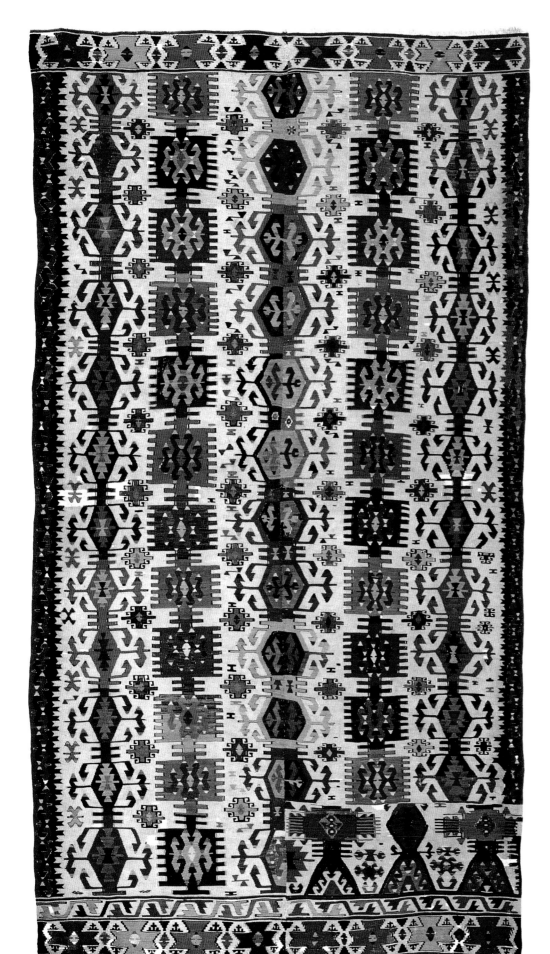

PLATE 16

AYDINLI-ZEBIR KILIM
Two-Piece

Size: 330 x 182 cm.

Warp: Wool, S plied   38/10 cm.

Weft: Wool, Z spun   140-240/10 cm (most is at the finer end of the scale).

Colours: Twelve – blue (dark to light), red, orange-red, turquoise, bluish green, pale yellow, aubergine, deep maroon, reddish brown, greyish brown, black, ivory.

Technique: Slit-tapestry; contour weft wrapping around the motifs has largely disappeared.

Condition: Good – it has had some repair.

The columnar motifs of this kilim are reminiscent of Hotamiş kilims woven near Konya (refer also to plate 24, *Flatweaves*, Balpinar and Hirsch). For the rest, the colours and the designs of side and end borders are very typical of Aydinli kilims. It is a well-matched two-piece kilim and the weaver has taken care to ensure that the colours of each motif on the one half correspond to the equivalent motif on the other. Therefore, it comes as a surprise to see the completely different set of figures that are included at one end of the field of one of the halves. Even the side border is different in this section. Obviously the weaver intended to make a kilim of a different design, but changed her mind shortly after beginning work.

PLATE 17
AYDINLI-ZEBIR KILIM

Size: 343 x 163 cm.

Warp: Wool, S plied   40/10 cm.

Weft: Wool, Z spun   260/10 cm.

Colours: Nine – blue (rubbed), madder red, brick red, turquoise, bluish green, pale green, aubergine, grey-brown, ivory.

Technique: Slit-tapestry with contour weft wrapping and soumak lines.

Condition: Very good.

This carefully worked, single-piece kilim is a village weaving from the Zebir area, a treeless plain with scattered salt marshes north of Konya. This region seems to be a rather formidable place for anyone to settle in. Several years ago one of the authors, while travelling back to Istanbul from Konya, met a university lecturer born in Zebir, who described how his ancestral group of the Aydinli tribe was fragmented through some political turmoil and fled westwards to those parts. They found the area harsh and inhospitable and had to dig wells to find potable water for themselves and their flocks but, as the land was uninhabited, they were at least left in peace. Splinter groups of the Karakeçili and Karakoyunlu tribes also sought refuge in the Zebir plains, remote even today from regular traffic. This kilim is a very sophisticated piece using lustrous wool. The weaving is very uniform and skilful; a real feature is made of the contour weft wrapping around the various components of the design.

PLATE 18

AYDINLI KILIM
Plain Field Dowry Cover; Two-Piece

Size: 400 x 183-189 cm.

Warp: Wool, S plied   37/10 cm.

Weft: Wool, Z spun   220/10 cm.

Colours: Fifteen – crimson, ox-blood red, brownish red, orange-red, blue, blue-green, olive green, lime yellow, mustard yellow, orange, yellowish orange, maroon, black, brown, ivory.

Technique: Slit-tapestry with some additional brocade figures and contour weft wrapping around most motifs.

Condition: Complete – it has some damage.

The preceding piece contrasts markedly with the kilim shown here. With its bold designs, strong colours and irregular weave, this one appeals because of its dynamic tribalism. Archetypal animalistic figures are prominent in the field design. One half is slightly more detailed and possesses a deeper and more interesting green. The central plain field is made up of bands of mainly reddish tones. It is woven in blocks or segments, subsequently introducing considerable numbers of lazy lines.

This piece had a particular function. At the end of a wedding ceremony, when the bride travelled to her new home, a camel selected to carry the dowry was bedecked with various trappings. This kilim was thrown over the dowry items – hence the plain central field and decorated ends, the last to fall along the camel's flanks and catch the eye as the animal swayed while it walked. Similar textiles are known from the Aleppo-Reyhanli and Fethiye regions (see also plate 31), but Aydinli dowry covers seem very rare indeed.

PLATE 19

AYDINLI KILIM
Two-Piece

Size: 335 x 185 cm.

Warp: Wool, S plied   43/10 cm.

Weft: Wool, Z spun; some metallic thread
140-240/10 cm.

Colours: Twelve – red, crimson, brick red, blue, grey-blue, blue-green, olive green, mauve, straw, orange, dark brown, ivory.

Technique: Slit-tapestry with some contour weft wrapping and additional brocade motifs.

Condition: Good – it has had some repair.

Recognisable as an Aydinli kilim because of its large, hooked figures set against a white ground, this piece has, however, unusual side borders. A comparison of this kilim with plates 14 and 15 shows how the weaver has used the basic pattern to achieve a different effect. She has placed much more emphasis on the large hooks that extend from each hexagon by surrounding them with an extra border done in stripes of red and white. At the same time, she has developed her central figures into separate medallions, resulting in a totally different concept compared with, for example, plate 15. All spaces within the field are filled with minor motifs, each precisely drawn.

PLATE 20

AYDINLI KILIM
Two-Piece

Size: 327 x 156 cm.

Warp: Wool, S plied   47/10 cm.

Weft: Wool, Z spun   200-240/10 cm.

Colours: Thirteen – dark blue, light blue, rust red, bright red, pinkish red, lilac, yellow-green, blue-green, yellow-orange, straw, camel brown, mushroom, ivory.

Technique: Slit-tapestry with a few scattered brocade figures. Most motifs are outlined with contour weft wrapping.

Condition: Considering its age, generally good. Some of the brown has corroded, particularly along the edges.

The limpid colour and handle of this kilim give a semblance of great age. Two unusual features about this piece are the way in which the reciprocal hooks of the side borders have been developed into a sinuous line isolated from other elements of the design, and also the way in which the contour weft wrapping is, in many places, carried around only one warp in the verticals instead of the normal two. This is a process difficult to achieve without distorting the weaving.

PLATE 21

MANISA YÖRÜK PRAYER KILIM

Size: 184 x 128 cm.

Warp: Wool, S plied   39/10 cm.

Weft: Wool, Z spun   160/10 cm.

Colours: Nine – bright red, lighter red, maroon-red varying to brown, orange-red, deep blue, blue, yellow, orange yellow, white.

Technique: Slit-tapestry with some contour weft wrapping; some brocade figures. The warps at one end are plaited into heavy tassels.

Condition: Good.

Illustrated is a prayer kilim with a strong tribal appearance. It was probably woven by a woman from some nomadic group in the Manisa area. Turkic influences are prevalent, from the predominant use of deep blues and reds to the types of figures it contains, especially in its borders.

Although obviously based on a tree-of-life design, the motifs of the central panel are compressed and fragmented. The central axis of the tree, such as can be seen in plate 22, is still found here but the side branches are no longer evident. The weaver has relied on her extensive fantasy to compose the inner and outermost borders. She has assembled an interesting array of figures with no two alike in any column.

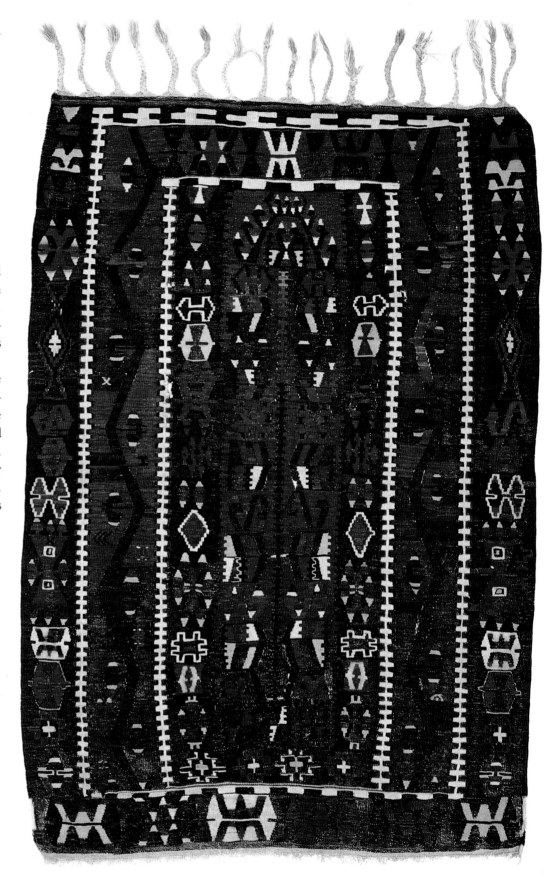

PLATE 22

AYDIN PRAYER KILIM

Size: 160 x 109 cm.

Warp: Cotton, S plied   44/10 cm.

Weft: Wool, Z spun   196/10 cm.

Colours: Nine – red (two shades), reddish maroon, orange, yellow, blue (rubbed), dark brown, muted aubergine, white.

Technique: Slit-tapestry with numerous small eccentric wefted motifs inset in it; contour weft wrapping surrounds many motifs.

Condition: Good.

In the region between Aydin and Uşak, various groups made prayer kilims which commonly incorporated the tree-of-life design. This is a very old symbol, widely used in Muslim countries, but originating in much earlier times. Stylised trees of life can be seen, for example, on bas-reliefs from Nimrud, dating from the Assyro-Babylon period, circa 900 BC.

In the designs of the tree is a hidden symbolism associated with the spiritual philosophy of Islamic mystical orders. One of the meanings of the dominating and explosive flower-like symbol at the base of the tree, as seen here, is undoubtedly God, or Allah, the source of all life. Note that at the end of each pair of side branches the terminating hooks point inwards, except on the fourth pair, where they point outwards. In many mystical orders there are four stages in reaching total enlightenment – three stages towards surrender of the self to God, and the final stage of spiritual illumination.

In diverse cultures there are many ways of using the tree-of-life design to illustrate basic religious beliefs. But how much more dynamic is the design shown here than the bastardised form, so commonly seen in rugs, of a flower decoration springing from a vase!

The Turkic origin of this particular kilim is especially evident from the borders – the sinuous line, complete with latch-hooks, progressing into end borders with the "running dog" pattern, as well as the extra borders at each end.

PLATE 23

BANAZ UŞAK PRAYER KILIM

Size: 188 x 159 cm.

Warp: Wool, S plied   39/10 cm.

Weft: Wool, Z spun; two strands are inserted together in some places   160/10 cm.

Colours: Nine – light blue, three reds, green, mustard yellow, mauve, dark brown, ivory.

Technique: Slit-tapestry with contour weft wrapping plus additional brocade motifs; eccentric weft inserts are a feature of this kilim.

Condition: The ends have been restored and there are some other repairs.

The prayer kilim in the accompanying plate is another based on the tree-of-life design. It is attributed to weavers from the region of Banaz, a small town lying between Uşak and Afyon.

This piece has an unusual configuration, from its squarish format to the arrangement of the components that make up the tree of life. The figure representing the explosion of life, seen at the base of the tree in plate 22, here occupies the central position of the mihrab. The tree projects beyond the ornate peak of the mihrab. Its branches terminate in stylised floral devices often referred to as tulips, which can also be seen in some prayer kilims from the Ladik region.

The colours of this kilim are also somewhat uncommon, particularly the quality of the green, the soft blue and the pronounced yellow.

PLATE 24

DAZKIRI KILIM

Size: 206 x 114 cm.

Warp: Wool, S plied   54/10 cm.

Weft: Wool, Z spun and cotton (white areas)   160/10 cm.

Colours: Seven – red, blue, deep turquoise, yellow, mustard yellow, dark brown, white.

Technique: Alternating slit-tapestry, plain weft-faced stripes and brocaded stripes; eccentric weft inserts are a feature.

Condition: Good – one side has slight damage.

From early Selçuk times several Turkic tribes have ranged through the elevated plateaus and mountains in the Afyon-Dazkiri area. Their kilims, both in choice of colour and technique, are quite distinct. One of the distinguishing features is the way in which they tend to use designs of a largely angular or curvilinear nature, thus effectively eliminating vertical slits. Where verticals are found, they are usually on figures with short-stepped edges.

Although the two Dazkiri kilims illustrated (plates 24 and 25) are essentially quite different in pattern, their colours are almost identical. Both use cotton extensively for the white areas and have a further homogeneity through their inclusion of narrow strips of brocade running from edge to edge – bordering every row of motifs in the kilim shown here – and their tassels decorated with coloured wools.

PLATE 25

DAZKIRI KILIM

Size: 190 x 127 cm.

Warp: Wool, S plied   47/10 cm.

Weft: Wool, Z spun and cotton (white areas) 180–220/10 cm.

Colours: Seven – red, blue, greenish blue, yellow, straw, dark brown, white (cotton).

Technique: Eccentric wefted tapestry, eliminating slits; the motifs are outlined with extra eccentric wefts. At each end are brocaded bands.

Condition: Very good.

The curvilinear motifs of this kilim, outlined as they are with free-flowing eccentric wefts, are wonderfully set off against the predominant glowing madder red and greenish blue. The yellow used in Dazkiri kilims has a particularly pleasing quality, being of a pale lime-yellow tint.

Note the succession of colours at the ends of each kilim. The extremely attractive Dazkiri kilim on display in the Vakiflar Museum, Istanbul (reproduced on plate 80, *Flatweaves*, Balpinar and Hirsch), and other kilims we have seen from this area, have the same sequence. This again demonstrates how strongly traditions are retained, although the weavers can – and do – improvise in the design of the main field.

PLATE 26

AFYON KILIM

Size: 246 x 157 cm.

Warp: Wool, mainly white, plus a band of red and brown, S plied   28/10 cm.

Weft: Wool, Z spun   120–130/10 cm.

Colours: Six – blue, red, yellow, pale lime green, brown, white.

Technique: Slit-tapestry with bands of brocade; eccentric weft-wrapping around the motifs.

Condition: Very good.

The kilim illustrated here has some features in common with the Dazkiri pieces just discussed, notably the angular motifs and the use of narrow strips of brocade to separate the bands of tapestry weave. However, the colours and weave place it further north towards Afyon. The original name of this town is Afyonkarahisar which translates literally as "opium black castle". The wefts of this piece are thick and tightly spun, and in spite of being firmly beaten down they barely cover the warps. This gives the kilim a pleasant textured effect, as well as making it very robust. Eccentric weft outlining performs an important function by accentuating the designs.

PLATE 27

ÇINE KILIM

Size: 132 x 104 cm.

Warp: Wool, S plied   47/10 cm.

Weft: Wool, Z spun   220/10 cm.

Colours: Eleven – red, lilac blue, mauve (varying to grey), yellow, straw yellow, two shades of orange, dark green, pale green, bluish black, ivory.

Technique: Slit-tapestry with some contour weft wrapping around most motifs.

Condition: It has had some repair.

Between Aydin and Muğla is found the small town of Çine, which has lent its name to some remarkably finely executed kilims. Probably woven by nomads who once roamed the mountains east of Çine, these pieces today are extremely rare.

Of the three pieces illustrated (plates 27 to 29), this one is the smallest and has the least densely packed wefts. However, the wool is of superior quality and possesses a beautiful lustre. These features, together with its vigorous designs and strong colours, make this is a weaving with considerable visual impact.

PLATE 28

ÇİNE KİLİM
Two-Piece

Size: 309 x 164 cm.

Warp: Wool, S plied   45/10 cm.

Weft: Wool, Z spun   280-340/10 cm.

Colours: Fourteen – red, orange-red, bright orange, brown, maroon, deep blue, lighter blue, blue-green, yellow, khaki (small amount), burnt umber, deep brownish black, plum black, ivory.

Technique: Slit-tapestry with some eccentric weft outlining.

Condition: Good – there has been repair of one corner plus some other small repairs.

Many of the motifs seen in the preceding kilim have also been used by the weaver of this piece, although in a modified form. The figures seen in the outer border of plate 27 are used here for the end borders but developed much more ornately; they are greatly simplified in the side borders. In this kilim the hexagonal motifs containing hooked figures are more precisely drawn.

The quality of the weave of this kilim is extraordinary. The lustrous wool has been spun very finely and is tightly packed, enabling the weaver to obtain such evident precision in the drawing of her figures. Colour combinations are exquisite and harmonious, and enhanced by the selected wools the weaver has worked with. Despite its size, the kilim's halves are perfectly matched.

PLATE 29

ÇINE KILIM
Two-Piece

Size: 407 x 158 cm.

Warp: Mohair, S plied   55/10 cm.

Weft: Mohair, Z spun   360-380/10 cm.

Colours: Nine – blue, dark grey-blue, brick red, maroon-red, orange-red, blue-green, deep aubergine, plum black, ivory.

Technique: Slit-tapestry weave.

Condition: Some of the dyes are corrosive.

In spite of its large size this very old kilim is the most finely woven of all those shown in this book. One cannot begin to imagine how long it must have taken the women to spin the materials for this kilim, made entirely of mohair, let alone weave it. The use of mohair imparts to it a different feel compared with wool, and instead of the silky lustre of woollen weaves, it has a glass lustre.

The designs are very clear-cut and exact, qualities the weaver was able to achieve through the use of such finely spun thread. The precision of the weaving has allowed the weaver to make many of the vertical slits between blocks of adjacent colours longer than usual but this has not weakened the textile to any degree. The visible damage to this piece has been brought about not by wear, but by corrosion and break-down of some of the colours, particularly some of the dark maroon and black. Further damage has occurred along the fold lines, for this kilim must have spent much of its lifetime stored away.

The overall design is intriguing; is it meant to be a dowry cover like the pieces shown in plates 18 and 31? With some semblance of a plain field in the centre of the weaving, it has this aspect. For the most part, the motifs found in this kilim are quite different from any we have seen in other weavings. The beautifully executed end borders, with their reciprocal pattern, however, are similar to those found in some of the Aydinli kilims, such as those shown in plates 16, 17 and 19.

PLATE 30

AYDINLI-FETHIYE KILIM

Size: 418 x 162 cm.

Warp: Wool, S plied   51/10 cm.

Weft: Wool, Z spun, cotton for white areas
160-260/10 cm.

Colours: Twelve – four reds, bright blue, pale blue,
salmon, olive brown, pale green, yellow, aubergine,
white (cotton).

Technique: Slit-tapestry weave with remains of contour
weft wrapping around most figures; some weft float
brocade motifs.

Condition: Fair – the light brown wool shows
considerable corrosion.

The main design is strongly Aydinli in character,
but the central column of hooked figures is very
much a feature found in kilims from the mountainous regions north of Fethiye. As mentioned
earlier, the Aydinli tribal group had a very extensive range and the people who made this
kilim possibly were influenced by Fethiye
weavings.

When procured, this piece was exceedingly
dirty. The freshness of the colours, with, in particular, the subtlety of use of the many shades
of red, was only revealed after careful washing.
The cotton used in the white ground is very
felted, a feature associated with considerable age.
Despite the damage this kilim has sustained
through the corrosion of the olive brown, it is
sufficiently complete to appreciate its beauty.

A similar kilim is illustrated in plate 35 of
Flatweaves, by Balpinar and Hirsch.

PLATE 31

FETHIYE DOWRY COVER

Size: 320 x 158 cm.

Warp: Wool, S plied   41/10 cm.

Weft: Wool, Z spun   220/10 cm.

Colours: Nine – red, pale red, blue, greenish blue, mustard yellow, orange, pale orange, dark brown, white.

Technique: Slit-tapestry with eccentric weft outlining plus a few brocade figures in the plain field.

Condition: Good – it has had minor repairs.

In the jumble of mountain ranges between Aydin and Antalya are found valleys and small plains, many of which are quite isolated. Groups of nomads have wandered through these parts and grazed their flocks here for centuries. Their weavings are quite distinctive in design and colouration. Some are labelled Fethiye after a small and picturesque town on the coast. It must be recognised that this is again a name of convenience, because it inadequately describes the tribespeople and does not define the extent of the territory that they covered in their migrations.

The dowry cover in plate 31 possesses many of these properties, in design and colouration as well as wool quality, that distinguish Fethiye-area kilims. However, plain field pieces of this type are quite rare now (compare also plate 18). The warps are finely spun although not densely packed. They are made of rather strong wool with a silky sheen. By organising her composition so that most lines are on a diagonal axis, the weaver has managed to avoid vertical slits to a large extent. The four hexagonal güls containing the white hooked figures all look very similar, but the weaver has purposely varied the fill-in motif of one of them. On the rich madder-red central field she has inserted two small brocade figures, almost as if they were a signature.

PLATE 32

FETHIYE ÇUVAL

Size: 117 x 80 cm.

Warp: Wool, S plied   52/10 cm.

Weft: Wool, Z spun in plain weave areas   180/10 cm; two strands are used together in design areas, plus cotton for white details.

Colours: Eight – blue, madder red, rust red, turquoise, yellow, orange, dark brown, white (cotton).

Technique: The design bands are composed of countered soumak brocade alternating with narrow strips of plain and slit-tapestry kilim; these in turn are delineated with rows of 1:1 brocade executed in dark brown and white; there are scattered brocade motifs near the mouth of the bag, front and rear; the reverse side is woven in different-coloured bands of plain kilim; two rows of cloth ornaments decorate the face of the bag.

Condition: Good, except for one hole.

Special Notes: The bag has two side straps woven of goat hair and cotton; on the face is a tuft of human (?) hair as an extra ornamentation.

Turkmen nomads, with their colourfully accoutred camels, are still to be seen in this region, as are also occasional glimpses of encampments of black tents. The sheep they herded must have been well bred because earlier weavings are made with wool of superior quality. Orange and yellow are used lavishly. In older pieces, both colours possess rich, mellowed tones. The orange is especially beautiful; it has the appearance of being brushed with burnt umber. From the nature of these two colours and the changes they undergo with time, it would appear that dyer's sumac was a common source of the dye. This small tree is one of the dominant species in the undergrowth of some of the mountain slopes in the area.

Looking at the dowry cover illustrated in plate 31, one can see the similarity in colouration of the çuval shown alongside. The dyes are especially rich and wonderfully mellowed by time. The back of the bag likewise is woven with these same splendid colours.

White cotton has also been used here to outline and emphasise the güls. Note the elibelinde ("hands on hips") motifs worked in this material. Altogether, this is an ornately decorated çuval which must have taken the weaver considerable time to make.

PLATE 33

DOŞEMEALTI ÇUVAL

Size: 128 x 76 cm.

Warp: Strong white wool, S plied   64/10 cm.

Weft: Wool, Z spun for plain weave areas 180-200/10 cm; two strands are used together for the design areas; cotton is used for the white; some camel hair.

Colours: Ten – blue, deep turquoise, green, madder red, burgundy red, orange, light brown, dark brown, camel, white (cotton).

Technique: Three main bands and four minor ones of mixed soumak brocade, separated by bands of plain weave in different colours, in which are woven narrow lines of two-colour zili; the back consists of bands of plain weave in different colours, with some rows of scattered brocade motifs.

Condition: Excellent.

Special Notes: A blue bead decorates the front of the bag.

The çuval illustrated is attributed to weavers from the Doşemealti tribal group, who occupied the mountain ranges closer to Antalya. The women in this area are famous for their weaving skills and today there is a considerable cottage industry of rug making around the village of Doşemealti, about 30 kilometres north of Antalya.

Although much more sombre in tone than the distinctly Fethiye-area çuvals, the colours here are nevertheless rich and mellow. The weaving is very skilful, the design areas being a combination of various zili techniques and soumak. The material used for the major elements of the design is quite crowded and many of the individual lines of soumak are applied eccentrically. This gives the effect of the motifs bursting from the face of the bag.

In spite of being an old çuval, both front and back are perfectly preserved. It has obviously been stored for several generations.

PLATE 33(a): By crowding the design wefts into the motif, the weaver has created an unusual effect. The blue bead is said to ward off the evil eye – detail of plate 33.

PLATE 34

KONYA-AKŞEHIR KILIM

Size: 182 x 111 cm.

Warp: Wool, S plied   39/10 cm.

Weft: Wool, Z spun   220/10 cm.

Colours: Nine – red, dark blue, lighter blue, yellow, pale green, pale lilac, bright orange, maroon, white.

Technique: Slit-tapestry with contour weft wrapping around some motifs.

Condition: Good.

Throughout the centuries numerous tribes settled on the plains around Konya, bringing with them diverse traditional designs and weaving skills. This occupation of the land, especially to the east and south-east of Konya, occurred voluntarily or was sometimes enforced by the Ottoman rulers. As towns and villages sprang up, many groups kept their identities intact, living in separate areas and often continuing to produce their own particular style of weavings. The variety of flatweaves originating from Konya Province is immense.

From this rather bewildering array we present, in the next few pages, some examples. The piece shown in plate 34 was probably woven northwest of Konya, in the region of Akşehir. It is an outstanding example to illustrate how powerfully-designed kilims can appeal equally as well as refined ones. The bold hooked figures are drawn with precision. Coupled with a suitable variety and harmony of colour, plus sufficient variation of minor motifs to avoid monotony, this kilim has quite an impact. Here, nothing is superfluous; even the extra border at each end is necessary to provide a balance to the overall design. The additional colours of the threads used in the contour weft wrapping of this piece add significantly to its creative force.

PLATE 35

DERBENT PRAYER KILIM

Size: 197 x 112 cm.

Warp: Wool, S plied   33/10 cm.

Weft: Wool, Z spun; in some white areas two strands are used together   180/10 cm.

Colours: Nine – two reds, blue, yellow, straw yellow, chocolate brown, greyish brown, green, white.

Technique: Slit-tapestry weave. The warp ends are braided into a net at one end of the kilim.

Condition: Very good.

This simple prayer kilim has a pristine beauty. Found in the village of Derbent, about 80 kilometres west of Konya, it probably has a nomadic origin. The authors have seen only one other kilim of this type and it was fragmented. The weaving is rather coarse, the variety of motifs austere, yet it is attractive because of its earthy colours and its strength of design. Many features relate to textiles from Turkestan, including the basic red colour and the bands of soldati figures (resembling tuning forks in rows). The quality of the colours and wool, as well as the two white ground borders, suggest it could have been woven by a woman from the Aydinli tribe.

PLATE 36

KONYA KILIM
Detail

Size: 336 x 160 cm.

Warp: Wool, S plied   38/10 cm.

Weft: Wool, Z spun   180-260/10 cm.

Colours: Nine – madder red, blue, salmon, green, yellow, ochre, aubergine, dark brown, white.

Technique: Slit-tapestry weave with remains of contour weft wrapping around the motifs.

Condition: Side borders are missing; there is some damage to the remainder.

The elibelinde motif is the principal element of design in both this kilim and the one following, but in each the treatment is quite different. Here the weaver has used the archaic, undivided form of the motif, organised in rows which can be viewed both horizontally and as diagonals. The colours are wonderfully clear and mature. They are used quite randomly; that is, the weaver has made no attempt to create a pattern with her colours.

The detail shown represents approximately one-sixth of the total kilim. This being quite a large weaving, the colours and the design can both be better appreciated by showing only a part of it than by reproducing the whole kilim.

PLATE 37

KONYA KILIM

Size: 162 x 120 cm.

Warp: Wool, hair and cotton; mainly one strand of brown wool twisted around one strand of white mohair; a band of white plied mohair; a band of plied cotton warps S plied   41/10 cm.

Weft: Wool, white areas are cotton, S plied and unplied   260/10 cm.

Colours: Ten – bright red, orange-red, orange, yellow, blue, pale blue, deep green, yellow-green, brown, white (cotton).

Technique: Slit-tapestry with contour weft wrapping. Remains of some tufts of wool decorate the field.

Condition: Good.

Compared with the previous piece, this kilim is much less sophisticated. The weaver has used a variety of fibres for the warps – possibly her poor, simple lifestyle dictated what she could obtain, so she incorporated materials she had to hand. The individual motifs are well drawn but the way the weaver has varied the use of her colours in the main field, resulting in bands of unequal width, gives a very unusual effect. Note also how one side border is much wider than the other. The cotton used for the white areas is very compacted and felted with age.

PLATE 38

ALIBEYHÜYÜK KILIM

Size: 197 x 120 cm.

Warp: Mohair, S plied 53/10 cm.

Weft: Wool, Z spun   320/10 cm; some metallic thread is also used.

Colours: Eleven – bright red, dark red, light red, light blue, bluish green, light yellow, dark yellow, khaki, dark brown, white, dark grey (metallic).

Technique: Slit-tapestry with eccentric weft outlining plus numerous brocaded motifs. The warp ends are formed into tassels at one end.

Condition: Very good.

From Alibeyhüyük in the Çumra district, southeast of Konya, comes the exquisite piece shown here. The mohair warps and woollen wefts are beautifully spun. Every aspect of this kilim – the choice of materials, the technically superb weaving methods, its balanced harmony of colour and design – indicates that it was woven by a very experienced weaver. The manner in which the wefts flow with the contour of the designs, the extensive use of eccentric weft outlining of the figures, as well as the additional brocade motifs and silver metallic highlights, add to one's appreciation of the weaving. The quality of the red, blue and green are typical of kilims from this region. A very old piece, it was undoubtedly stored and treasured by a family for several generations before being sold.

PLATE 39

HOTAMIŞ ÇUVAL

Size: 145 x 101 cm.

Warp: Wool, S plied 79/10 cm.

Weft: Wool, Z spun for the plain weave areas 180-200/10 cm; design areas have three strands of Z spun wool used together; cotton is used for the white.

Colours: Ten – madder red, orange-red, bordeaux, blue, yellow, lime green, pale blue-green, brown, mauve, white (cotton).

Technique: The two panels of design are basically modified zili brocade (offset 2:2 floats), bordered by two-colour twining. Plain weave areas are worked in mainly yellow and red, with some blue.

Condition: Good.

Special Notes: Instead of the edges of the design areas being woven in plain weave, as is normal for Hotamiş çuvals, they are executed in over two under two weave, using multiple wefts, as in the design panels.

A few hundred years ago, groups of Turkic nomads from northern Syria occupied part of the southern extent of the huge steppes that stretch east and north of Konya. Now generally lumped together under the name Hotamiş, they have since settled down in the area, and southeast of Konya there is now a village bearing this name. The people we have met from this tribal group do not, however, refer to themselves as Hotamiş, but proudly call themselves Turkmen. The Hotamiş were accomplished weavers and brought to this part of Turkey a distinctive style of design and colour usage. Some of their çuvals are delightful. They can be distinguished usually by the way the pattern is not woven from edge to edge. Instead the edges are filled in with bands of alternating colours, as can be seen in the çuval illustrated. Note the warm, harmonising colours of this piece, which are carried through to the precisely drawn strap. Even the embroidered overbinding of the strap is worked in the same colours.

PLATE 40

KARAPINAR KILIM

Size: 431 x 158 cm.

Warp: Wool, mostly white except for a 16 cm band of light brown on one edge, S plied   38/10 cm.

Weft: Wool, Z spun   140-260/10 cm.

Colours: Ten – blue, blue-green, green, orange-red, madder red, brownish red, orange, dark reddish brown, walnut brown, ivory.

Technique: Slit-tapestry weave. The motifs are outlined by eccentric wefts. There are numerous extra brocade figures. At one end the warp loops are held together by a thick cord running through them; at the other end the warps are knotted together in groups and formed into tassels (mostly unravelled).

Condition: Good, except for some corrosion of the walnut brown.

Karapinar kilims take several different forms. This one is a classic type much sought after by collectors. Made by one of the many groups of Yörüks who have now settled in and around Karapinar, which is situated about 70 kilometres east of Konya, it encompasses both a strength of design and bold colours that make it instantly eye-catching. The quality of the colours used in these early pieces is superb, from the rubbed appearance of the indigo blue, the green created by overdyeing yellow with blue, with the yellow showing through in varying amounts, to the rich reds and deep maroon. The overall design and succession of the colours used for the medallions of this type of kilim is invariable; where the weaver is able to use her creative abilities and artistry is in the minor figures inserted along the sides. Some pieces, particularly more recent ones, turn out to be very static, but the one illustrated here shows wonderful improvisations, a feast of exciting shapes and colours.

PLATE 41

KARAPINAR ÇUVAL

Size: 115 x 93 cm.

Warp: Wool, S plied   49/10 cm.

Weft: Wool, Z spun   220-260/10 cm.

Colours: Ten – madder red, bright red, orange-red, aubergine, blue, blue-green, straw yellow, brown, lighter brown, ivory.

Technique: The brocading is mostly cicim, with some modified zili brocade (offset 2:2 floats) executed in several stripes and separated by plain weave in different colours. Each band of brocade was bordered by two-colour twining, little of which remains. The back is plain weft-faced weave in white wool.

Condition: Good.

Special Notes: The design panel was woven separately from the remainder of the çuval.

This large çuval is also attributed to the Karapinar area. Unlike many of the pieces illustrated, it is very limited in its range of colours, relying instead on slight shifts of colour temperature. The total effect is one of harmony, which is further achieved by the skilful weaving and use of glossy wool. An interesting feature which we have observed in many çuvals is that yellow, one of the easiest natural dyes to obtain, is only sparingly used.

PLATE 42
OBRUK KILIM

Size: 376 x 123 cm.

Warp: Wool, S plied   58/10 cm.

Weft: Wool, Z spun   200-270/10 cm.

Colours: Ten – madder red, ox-blood red, maroon, blue, bluish green, pale green, aubergine, dark brown, white, walnut.

Technique: Slit-tapestry weave.

Condition: Very good.

Kilims from the Obruk area, especially the prayer type, are renowned. An extensive yayla (grazing ground) north-east of Konya, in the past used by several tribal groups, the area has now been settled. This yayla is a vast, virtually treeless plain reminiscent of the Russian steppes. It is still the centre of a variety of weavings, including brocades of different kinds. The village of Obruk itself is a small market centre and should not be considered the source of so-called Obruk weavings.

This fine and skilfully woven runner is made from soft, lustrous wool. It feels very light and thin. Note the precision in the composition of the figures. Although an old piece, it has obviously been stored away carefully for many decades, so it still has a new appearance; such kilims as these are now quite rare and eagerly sought after by collectors.

Significant of this kilim and others of this type that we have seen is that there is generally an absence of outlining of the motifs by additional wefts, as is found in most other kilims of western and central Anatolia.

PLATE 43

OBRUK ZILI

Size: 161 x 120 cm.

Warp: Wool, purple-brown, S plied   90/10 cm.

Weft: Wool, Z spun; cotton is used for white areas; ground weave   90/10 cm.

Colours: Ten – crimson red, red, orange-red, blue, olive green, pale olive green, red-brown, greyish brown, white (cotton) – against the purple-brown of the ground weave.

Technique: Basically 3:3 zili on a balanced ground weave. At one end the warps are plaited into tassels.

Condition: Good.

A strong Turkoman influence can be seen in the zili shown alongside. Eight-pointed stars enclosed in octagons are found in a very early Anatolian rug, dating from about 1400, as well as later examples from the Caucasus. The güls of some Tekke Turkoman rugs are based on a similar concept, but generally they are not so angular. The emblematic significance of the güls in this zili is made more evident by the use of white cotton to surround the stars so that they stand out clearly. With their long fringes at one end and lack of fringes at the other, such pieces as these are obviously designed as hangings – in some cases, small loops for attaching them to walls are added to the end without fringes (see also plate 45).

PLATE 44

ASAĞIPINARBAŞI PRAYER KILIM

Size: 186 x 125 cm.

Warp: Wool, light and dark strands twisted together, S plied   45/10 cm.

Weft: Wool, Z spun, plus cotton in white areas 240/10 cm.

Colours: Eleven – bright red, orange-red, maroon, deep blue, mauve, yellow, blue-green, light green, straw, dark brown, white (cotton).

Technique: Slit-tapestry, with some contour weft wrapping, plus scattered brocade motifs.

Condition: Excellent.

There are many Obruk prayer kilims with a basic format similar to this piece, but very few are as stylish or as beautiful. Woven in the village of Asağipinarbaşi, west of Obruk and only 35 kilometres north of Konya, it contains design elements distinctive of this village in the upper half of its field. The green used here and in the last piece discussed is peculiar to the Obruk region. Note also the rich brownish red of the field, similar to the ground colour used in some old Turkoman rugs, and the way the mihrab is delineated with white cotton. It is rare to find an old kilim from this area in such good condition.

PLATE 45

KEÇIMUHSINE CICIM

Size: 159 x 126 cm.

Warp: Wool, S plied   66/10 cm.

Weft: Wool, ground weave S plied   180/10 cm; for the design wefts, three strands of Z spun wool are used together.

Colours: Ten – red, maroon-red, pinkish red, blue, dark turquoise, yellow (one small area), brown, olive brown, mauve, white.

Technique: Overall cicim brocade on a white balanced ground weave.

Condition: Very good.

The prayer rug shown in this plate is from Keçimuhsine, about 35 kilometres north-west of Konya. It consists mainly of small boteh figures executed in cicim technique on a balanced plain weave. Side and end borders as well as the framing of the mihrab are, however, worked in offset zili. Although similar textiles were woven in the Obruk and Karapinar regions, this particular type, with its white background and minor motifs, is distinctly Keçimuhsine in origin; such rugs have been made in this ancient village for centuries. Usually only three cypresses are found placed along the vertical axis. The inclusion of two additional motifs of this kind, as in this weaving, is a rare feature. For Islamic Sunni mystical orders the cypress was a symbol with an intricate religious significance. Many gravestones, especially in the Konya region, are adorned with a green-painted cypress. Additional decorations in the form of tufts of wool and even strips of cloth, many now mere remnants, were attached to the sides of this piece. A further row of woollen strands, also greatly worn away, was inserted just above the fringes. The remains of some cloth decorations can be found along the central axis.

PLATE 46

KONYA-AKSARAY KILIM

Size: 463 x 158 cm.

Warp: Wool, S plied   44/10 cm.

Weft: Wool, Z spun; some cotton in white areas 200/10 cm.

Colours: Eleven – blue (rubbed), two reds, cochineal red, yellow, orange, green (blue and yellow are distinct), reddish brown, dark plum brown, ivory, white (cotton).

Technique: Slit-tapestry with contour weft wrapping.

Condition: Good – much of the brown is restored.

Through its use of bold hooked figures and appealing colour combinations, the large kilim woven in one piece shown here commands attention. The old colours have taken on a wonderful quality, seen most notably in the green, which on close examination appears largely made up of interspersed strands of blue and yellow. This has been brought about by the varying degrees of mellowing of the dyed wool, originally yellow overdyed with blue. The white wool has turned quite yellow with age, in contrast with the patches of cotton, which have remained white, although now very matted.

This kilim was probably woven by women of an Aydinli tribal group, although it also has many similarities to kilims of the Hotamiş people.

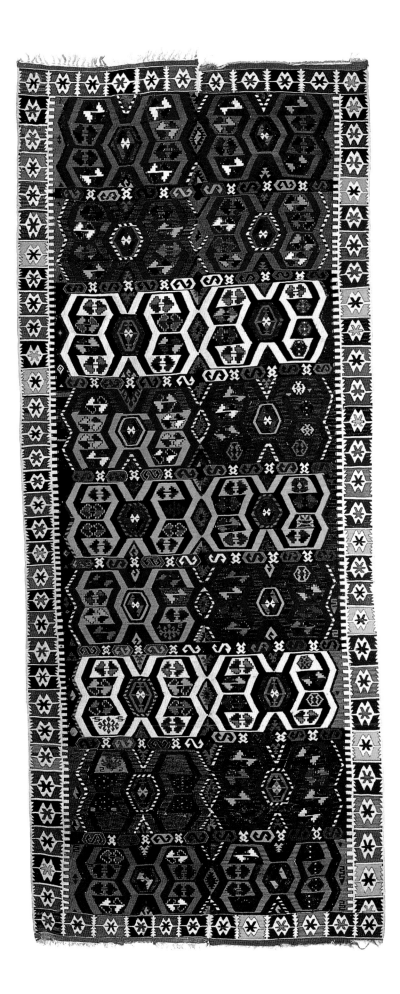

PLATE 47

AKSARAY KILIM
Two-Piece

Size: 396 x 163 cm.

Warp: Wool, S plied   49/10 cm.

Weft: Wool, Z spun, two strands used together, cotton in some white areas   240-280/10 cm; there is also one small patch of silver metallic thread.

Colours: Fifteen – blue, pale blue, grey, brick red, crimson, yellow, green, olive green, pale green, khaki, orange, mauve, dark reddish brown, ivory, white (cotton).

Technique: Slit-tapestry with contour weft wrapping. The warp ends have been knotted in bundles of ten.

Condition: Very good.

Its harmonious colours and balanced design make this carefully executed two-piece kilim very attractive. It surely is no accident that the centre of the field is worked in a rich golden yellow; from this focal point one's eye roves outwards to encompass the wealth of colour in the rest of the field. Much of the white in the design is woven using white wool, which has become ivory-coloured with age, but where the emphasis is placed on the two panels delineated in white in the central field, cotton has been used instead. As is also typical of many kilims from the Konya area, pale aubergine is juxtaposed with blue in some of the figures. This piece was undoubtedly highly regarded by the several generations who cared for it since its manufacture, for it has seen little use and seemingly only the reverse side was ever exposed. This side is slightly more faded than the face of the kilim. We have observed that other fine old pieces have been respected by being used on the reverse side only.

PLATE 48

YASTIK

Size: 77 x 45 cm.

Warp: Cotton, dyed blue   110/10 cm.

Weft: The ground field wefts are cotton, dyed blue 90/10 cm; the design wefts are finely spun S plied wool, two strands of which are used together, plus cotton for the white areas.

Colours: Nine – blue, red, maroon, reddish brown, dark brown, bright yellow, pale yellow, orange, white (cotton).

Technique: Most of the design area is 3:1 zili, offset to achieve diagonal designs, plus some soumak for the horizontals; cicim motifs are used for the borders as well as the back of the yastik – the whole against a balanced ground weave of blue cotton. The back of the cushion is woven as a separate piece. One set of warps at each end is twisted together to form long tassels. Some tufts of mohair decorate the front of the cushion.

Condition: Very good.

Also from the Konya region is the yastik shown alongside. This piece is unusual in that both the warps and ground wefts are made of blue-dyed cotton. Much skill has gone into the weaving of this cushion. The back of it is also ornamented with an overall design in cicim brocade. The extra embellishments, such as the tufts of coloured mohair that decorate the field, and the long tassels, as well as the careful binding of the edges with different-coloured wools, all point to the pride the weaver took in her weaving. As an indication of the high regard in which this piece was held in the weaver's family, during the limited use it was given it was turned inside out so that the brocade designs of both the face and the back have been protected.

PLATE 49

YASTIK

Size: 180 x 39 cm.

Warp: Wool, S plied 68/10 cm.

Weft: Wool, S plied for the ground weave 60/10 cm; two unplied Z spun strands are inserted together for the brocade.

Colours: Six – blue, red, deep bordeaux, black, orange, ivory (ground weave).

Technique: Mainly countered soumak on a balanced plain weave, but mixed with contour zili. The back has scattered motifs in contour zili against the balanced plain weave. Forming an edge to the main panel on the front are rows of two-colour twining giving a chain-weave effect.

Condition: Good.

Compared with the cushion illustrated in plate 48, this one has quite a different effect on our visual senses, not only because of its different pattern and technique, but also because of its more limited use of colours. The colours, however, are nicely balanced and, together with its very stylish design, provide it with considerable charm. It was also once decorated with a row of coloured tufts, but these have been largely worn away. We are not absolutely sure of its provenance and it could well be from the region of Sivas, although it has some attributes of Konya-area weavings.

PLATE 50

SIVRIHISAR PRAYER KILIM

Size: 210 x 127 cm.

Warp: Wool, S plied   37/10 cm.

Weft: Wool, Z spun; in some places two strands are used together   180/10 cm.

Colours: Eight – three reds, blue (rubbed), pale lime green, terracotta, pale olive brown, ivory.

Technique: Slit-tapestry; eccentric weft outlining of the figures has mostly disappeared; a few extra brocade motifs.

Condition: It has had some repairs; one side and one end are restored.

About halfway between Ankara and Afyon lies the small town of Sivrihisar, which has lent its name to a great number of kilims made by the many groups of nomads who once roamed the plains and ranges in its district. The kilims from this region can usually be recognised by their looser weave, their recurring motifs and especially their colours. A particular shade of salmon, wine red, pale olive brown, pale lime green and muted aubergine are frequently encountered.

Plate 50 shows an early example which includes many of the characteristics of a tribal group found south-east of Sivrihisar. A multi-niche prayer kilim, a form that is quite common for the Sivrihisar area, it has patterns in the border often referred to as tombs or yürts (the dome-shaped felt tents of the Turkomans). These suggestions as to the origins of the design are, at best, speculative. As is the case with many kilim designs, their significance is unknown, their original meaning having been lost over the ages.

PLATE 51

SIVRIHISAR KILIM

Size: 397 x 162 cm.

Warp: Wool, S plied   40/10 cm.

Weft: Wool, Z spun   220-280/10 cm.

Colours: Ten – madder red, orange-red, blue, grey, aubergine, mauve, olive green, orange, black, ivory.

Technique: Slit-tapestry; most figures are outlined with contour weft wrapping.

Condition: It has some damage.

Apart from its design, the weave and pale colours of this piece are typical of Sivrihisar-area kilims as a whole. Large kilims from this region, like the one illustrated, are not common. Although this is a very old piece, some of the colours are brighter than is normal for this area of Turkey, but particular shades and the texture of the weave help place it as having been woven in these parts. The boldly designed latch-hook side borders are a feature found in other Sivrihisar kilims. Note the serpentine Turkoman line running through each end border. The elibe-linde motif that makes up the field is of the archaic form (compare plates 36 and 37).

PLATE 52

HAYMANA KILIM

Size: 482 x 175 cm.

Warp: Wool, S plied   52/10 cm.

Weft: Wool, Z spun; cotton is used in the white areas   180/10 cm.

Colours: Eight – blue, turquoise, red, maroon, green, orange, dark chocolate brown, white (cotton).

Technique: Slit-tapestry with eccentric weft outlining around some figures; there are also scattered additional brocade motifs. At one end the warps show remains of having been braided into a net.

Condition: It has suffered some damage.

South-east of Ankara can be found a small range of mountains whose highest peak, Elmadaği (Apple Mountain), has given its name to a small town nearby. Spreading to the south-west of this range is the vast yayla of Haymana. It was on these plains that some nomadic groups once found pasture for grazing. The kilims they produced were very distinctive in their design, colour and, in some cases, their immensity. Little is known today of the people who made these so-called Haymana kilims. All extant pieces, as far as we have seen, are old, suggesting that Turkic nomads of the past settled down long ago to an agricultural existence and ceased weaving. Kurds later penetrated some areas to take over the vacated pastures. Now they, too, have become settled.

Many people in the trade used to ascribe large single-piece kilims, such as that shown in the accompanying plate, to the Dazkiri region. Now, with the increased awareness in kilims as more of the old pieces have come to light, most would agree that their origin is indeed the Haymana yayla. Most of these large kilims were made with finely spun warps – this piece, in spite of being the largest one we have included in this book, is one of the finest in terms of warping. With its clarity of design and wonderful range of matured vegetable dyes, especially the quality of the green with the yellow showing through, it is very striking. The cotton which is used for the white areas is very felted, an indication of the great age of this kilim.

PLATE 53

HAYMANA KILIM

Size: 212 x 115 cm.

Warp: Wool, S plied   45/10 cm.

Weft: Wool, Z spun, plus cotton for the white areas   170/10 cm.

Colours: Seven – red, pale maroon, blue, orange-yellow, green, brown, white (cotton).

Technique: Slit-tapestry with some extra brocade motifs; some eccentric weft outlining. The warps are braided into a small net at one end.

Condition: Good.

Special Notes: Three tufts of different-coloured wool decorate the centre of the field.

The Turkoman influence runs strong in all three kilims illustrated from the Haymana region, from the particular rich maroon-red – forming the background of the mihrab in the following plate – to the rows of soldati or arrowhead figures found in each. The impressive main border at each end of plates 52 and 53 is very commonly used in this category of Haymana kilims. It is, in fact, a composite development of the end borders seen in kilims such as plates 2 or 40.

A very typical feature of Haymana kilims is the use of cotton for certain motifs in the design. This kilim has rather more than normal, the cotton usually being confined to a few figures in the main end borders, as in the previous plate. The whiteness of the cotton stands out starkly from the deep vegetable dyes of the remainder of the field.

PLATE 54

ELMADAĞ PRAYER KILIM

Size: 184 x 110 cm.

Warp: Brown wool; on one side there is a band of one brown and one white strand plied together; S plied   43/10 cm.

Weft: Wool, Z spun, cotton for some white areas 240/10 cm.

Colours: Ten – red, maroon-red, blue, lime green, pale yellow, orange, bright yellow, reddish brown, ivory, white (cotton).

Technique: Slit-tapestry with some eccentric weft outlining; there are brocaded figures at both ends. The warps at one end are braided and plaited into a net.

Condition: Good.

Whereas the main kilims from this region are normally referred to as Haymana, for some reason the prayer kilims are usually called Elma-dağ. These pieces are rare. The design of the kilim in plate 54 seems markedly different from the two other pieces shown, but there are many structural similarities, even though it most probably was made by a different group in the Haymana area. It is a very stylish kilim, the small motifs of the central field and the simplified mihrab being offset by the bolder designs of the borders. What gives it real charm, however, is the warmth of its colours. Like the other two kilims illustrated, the warp ends are braided into a lattice. Another feature, the signature of smaller Haymana kilims as it were, is the row of small multicoloured brocade figures at each end near the fringes. The kilim in plate 53 similarly bears this mark.

PLATE 55

ÇORUM PRAYER KILIM

Size: 131 x 85 cm.

Warp: Wool; a light brown strand is twisted together with a white strand; S plied   43/10 cm.

Weft: Wool, Z spun   360/10 cm.

Colours: Ten – blue, bright red, bluish red, yellow, lime green, orange, orange-yellow, purplish brown, dark brown, white.

Technique: Slit-tapestry weave with contour weft wrapping around some figures. The warp ends are plaited to form tassels.

Condition: The sides have been restored.

While perhaps not as old as most of the kilims illustrated in this book, the kilim shown alongside warrants inclusion because of its unusual design. The simple mihrab is greatly accentuated by the swollen octagonal figure that encloses it. The paired columns that support the arch seem to represent the similar structures in the mosque that bear the mihrab, or prayer niche, marking the direction in which worshippers must turn to face Mecca. Aspects of its weave and colouration, particularly the quality of the yellow and lime green, suggest that this kilim was woven in the vicinity of Çorum, north-east of Ankara.

In all, this piece has a certain rustic naivety, which is further emphasised by its uneven proportions.

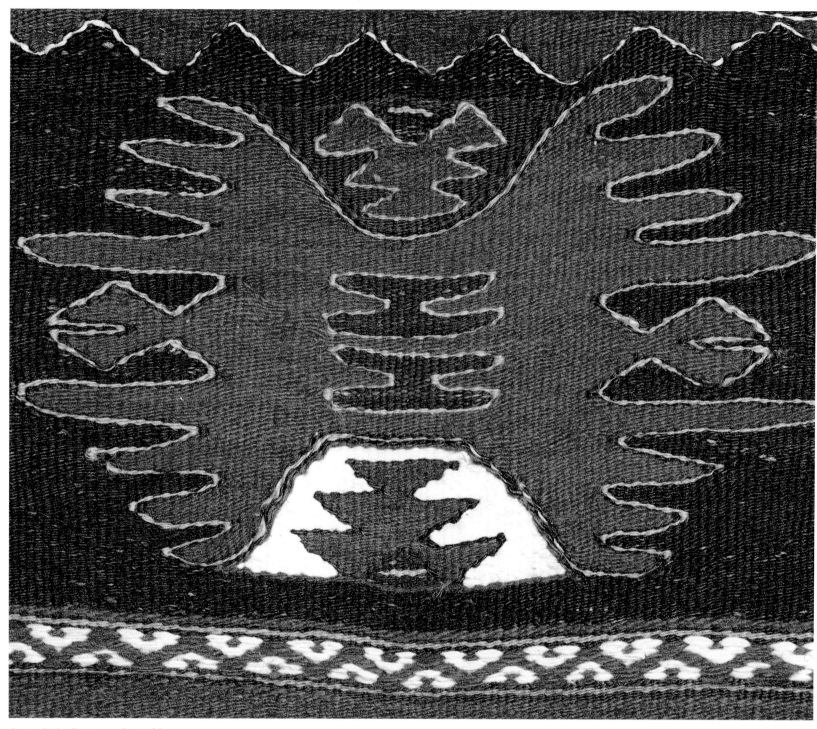

Plate 56A - Detail of Plate 25

The kilims of the Taurus Mountains, to the south and south-east of Konya, have a special fascination because of their strong tribal influences. Usually named after Mut, a small town situated in an important pass through the mountains between Konya and Silifke, the kilims were actually woven by nomads who ranged to the east and west of this pass. Turkoman traditions of usage of colours and designs have been retained in these weavings to a greater extent than in those from most other regions.

Turkic tribes migrated to the Taurus Mountains many centuries ago. Finding an environment resembling in many ways that of their ancestral homelands, with harsh winters and long dry summers, they settled into a life of migrating to the coastal lowlands for the winter and retreating to the mountain pastures over the summer period. The rugged nature of their adopted territory kept them isolated from other peoples and meant they could pursue their nomadic way of life unhindered for longer than in many other areas of Anatolia.

PLATE 56B - DETAIL OF PLATE 14

We have already described the struggles between the Yörük and the government forces which occurred in the last quarter of the 19th century. Since then the nomadic life has been in decline. But even today several thousand Yörüks persist in their seasonal migrations through these parts of the Taurus Mountains. For several years one of the authors was fortunate enough to intercept the caravans at an overnight resting camp in a defile which the nomads reached early in October. At daybreak the black tents are dismantled and packed inside çuvals. The camels are made to lie down, a large çuval is placed either side of each beast and the straps tied together across their backs. Further parcels, goatskins filled with water, cooking utensils, and so on, are tied on. Small children are placed in padded and protected parts of the luggage, the camels are instructed to stand and the caravan sets off on its way again. By this time the flocks of sheep and black goats are already far ahead along the route, since they depart at first light, accompanied by their shepherds.

Owing to the nature of the terrain the Yörüks traverse, it is not easy

PLATE 56C - DETAIL OF A NUZUMLA KILIM

to visit their winter camps. Since the coastal plains have been occupied by agricultural communities over the last hundred years, the Yörüks are confined to seeking winter quarters in sheltered valleys and milder southern slopes of the mountains. The last group, of about thirty camels, the author encountered was going to a remote area about 40 kilometres east of Mut. On an earlier occasion, he met a group on its way to overwintering grounds near the villages of Dikili and Sakran, southwest of Ermenek.

Government pressure on their way of living has taught the Yörüks to distrust any outside interference. They have always valued their independence, a feeling that persists to the present day. The Yörüks possess a deep pride in their traditions and origins, looking down on settled people. They speak in an old Turkic tongue maintained over the centuries since they migrated from the Khorasan to Anatolia. Urban Turks often have great difficulties understanding them.

Plate 56D

PLATE 57

MUT KILIM

Size: 275 x 130 cm.

Warp: Brown wool, S plied   33/10 cm.

Weft: Wool, Z spun   180-240/10 cm.

Colours: Four – madder red, blue, dark brown, ivory.

Technique: Slit-tapestry with eccentric weft outlining and eccentric weft inserts.

Condition: Good – it has had small amounts of repair.

It is this continuity of a basic lifestyle, reaching back millennia, where pride and dignity are more important than so-called progress and the clutter of possessions, that fascinates us. Nomadism is the oldest and most continuous form of human existence. The strength of character of the Yörüks of the Taurus Mountains around Mut is seen in their weavings. In old ones only a few colours occur, but the result of the strong elementary patterns can have a tremendous impact on our senses, as in the kilim featured here. Some people who have viewed this kilim at first hand find it disturbing, perhaps because of its archetypal, almost primeval arrangement of design and colour. For some reason it seems to affect men more than women.

Not surprisingly the colours are reminiscent of those used in weavings from Turkestan – madder red, blue, undyed white and brown wool. The whole weaving, virtually, is composed using one motif, a comb-like figure. The intricate and varied ways in which this motif is employed produces a fascinating composition, with a great interplay of reciprocality. Slits are almost completely eliminated by the use of angular designs, thus avoiding vertical lines.

There is little doubt that this kilim represents an archaic type, with its roots far back in the early traditions of the tribe. Much of its charm depends on the eccentric wefting, together with its simple yet effective colouration. The colours are variable – note the streaks of brown running through the red.

Some of its design elements could represent prototypes of figures found in old kilims from villages north of the Taurus Mountains and from other tribes. Compare, for example, the end border motif of this kilim (plate 56d) with the others shown in this series. All appear to have been developed from a common form.

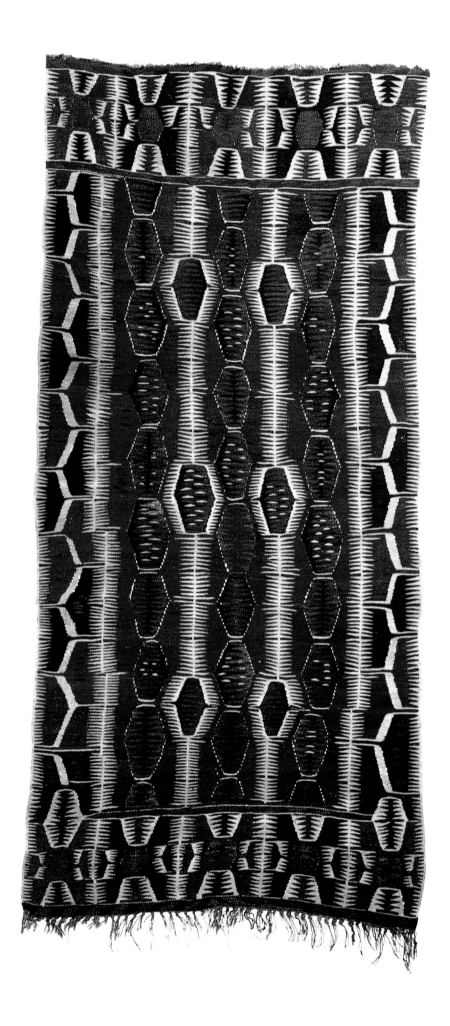

PLATE 58

MUT KILIM

Size: 269 x 111 cm.

Warp: Dark brown wool, S plied   32/10 cm.

Weft: Wool, Z spun   180-240/10 cm.

Colours: Seven – madder red, blue, green, aubergine, orange, brown, ivory.

Technique: Slit-tapestry weave, originally with eccentric weft outlining of most figures, much of which is worn away. The fringes are combined in bundles to form knotted tassels.

Condition: Very good.

Repetitive large ramshorn figures dominate this kilim, but the weaver has avoided monotony by randomly scattering numerous and varied small fill-in figures.

By mainly restricting the use of white to the motifs on the periphery, she has created the effect of a kilim with complete borders.

The quality of the colours and the wool are superb – altogether, this piece possesses an arresting dynamism.

 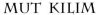

PLATE 59

MUT KILIM

Size: 236 x 114 cm.

Warp: Wool; a greyish brown and a camel brown strand are plied together; S plied   35/10 cm.

Weft: Wool, Z spun   200-240/10 cm.

Colours: Seven – madder red (sometimes varying to brownish red), coral red, blue, green (separated into blue and yellow), brown, yellow, ivory.

Technique: Slit-tapestry weave with a mixture of eccentric weft outlining and contour weft wrapping around the motifs. The warp ends are combined in bundles to form knotted tassels.

Condition: Very good.

The end borders and the toothed columnar fig-ures of the kilim illustrated have a clear relation-ship with the kilim in plate 57, but they are developed in a different style. Like those of the previous two pieces, the colours of this kilim are strong and beautiful. The interplay of the colours with their marked abrash, including the subtle usage of the two reds, gives this kilim a very cheerful aspect.

PLATE 60

MUT KILIM

Size: 170 x 93 cm.

Warp: Black goat hair, S plied   38/10 cm.

Weft: Wool, Z spun   200/10 cm.

Colours: Nine – red, blue, grey, orange-yellow, straw yellow, olive green, orange, dark brown, white.

Technique: Slit-tapestry weave.

Condition: Very good.

The piece shown here has warps made of lustrous black goat hair, quite a common feature of the so-called Mut weavings. Note the lovely interplay of reciprocal motifs in the lower border of this kilim. By concentrating on the white figures and then on the coloured ones in turn, separate motifs spring forth. The overall design of this piece is particular to this region and can also be found in large kilims of the same origin. This is a rather unusual feature because the composition of smaller kilims is generally quite different from larger ones.

PLATE 61

YAHYALI PRAYER KILIM

Size: 197 x 117 cm.

Warp: Wool, S plied   43/10 cm.

Weft: Wool, mixed plied and unplied   180-200/10 cm.

Colours: Nine – deep red, violet, orange, mustard yellow, grey, olive green, umber brown, dark brown, ivory.

Technique: Slit-tapestry weave.

Condition: Good – one end has been restored.

Some 90 kilometres south of Kayseri lies the small township of Yahyali. Here and in the surrounding villages there is quite a carpet-making industry. The carpets are generally well made but most have poor chemical colours. In the past also this area was involved in the manufacture of hand-knotted carpets, but it was the kilims for which it was renowned, particularly those of a prayer format.

As a general rule, Yahyali kilims have an extra panel above and below the mihrab or niche. The colours tend to be muted and subtle, with a preponderance of mustard yellow and reddish browns.

PLATE 62

YAHYALI PRAYER KILIM

Size: 186 x 125 cm.

Warp: Wool, S plied   46/10 cm.

Weft: Wool, mixed plied and unplied   160/10 cm.

Colours: Twelve – orange-red, deep red, blue, dark blue, mauve (varying to grey), yellow, umber, straw, pale green, brown, dark brown, ivory.

Technique: Slit-tapestry weave.

Condition: Reasonably good.

Centipede-like motifs are commonly dominant features in the design of the mihrab in Yahyali kilims. The borders contain only a few motifs, some very reminiscent of those used in kilims from north-eastern Turkey. However, the mihrab and field designs generally vary tremendously and are often very beautiful.

The weave is more relaxed than is customary for the kilims of most areas we have described up to now. Consequently the handle is softer and more supple. Note that the wefting material of both kilims shown consists of a mixture of plied and unplied wools; for some colours plied wool is used, for others unplied, although overall there is more of the former.

The broken, mountainous terrain of the eastern extension of the Taurus and subsidiary mountain chains, together with forcible settlement and relocation of peoples during Ottoman times, has had a tremendous effect on the composition of the populace of southern central Turkey. This has been compounded by the later squabbling between Turkey and Syria over defining the border.

Kilims described as Adana will not have been made in Adana itself, but in the Taurus Mountains to the north, which once harboured many groups of nomads. The present-day city of Adana, a hot, dusty and uninteresting place situated squarely in the Çukurova Plains, is the centre of considerable agricultural and industrial activity. Other kilims from this area are variously called Aleppo or Reyhanli. Aleppo (Halap or Halep), a city in Syria, near its border with Turkey, was once an important trading post of the Ottoman Empire. It is famous for its bazaar. Due north of Aleppo is the Turkish township of Gaziantep, a name which is also sometimes given to weavings from the south-east.

The term Reyhanli, as applied to kilims, can cause confusion. Reyhanli is a small town inside Turkey, almost on the Syrian border. It is named after the Reyhanli tribe, some groups of which used to make a seasonal migration extending as far north as Sivas. As the Reyhanli tribe splintered and settled, two major groups of their weavings could be recognised – those, often large, and using design panels with a squarish format, from near Sivas, and those from the Gaziantep-Aleppo region, with their distinctive southern palette.

Whatever names are used to describe kilims from this area, they have a certain unity of materials and weave, and particularly of colour. These kilims possess a spectrum of hues not found elsewhere, and one can see in them wine reds and cochineal replacing the deep madder reds used in most other areas, blues ranging into lighter, more limpid shades, and an unusual olive green. Altogether, their colours are made up of more intermediate shades and, with their common extensive use of cotton for the white areas of design, their appearance is lighter and brighter than the weavings of other Turkic tribes in Turkey, which are dominated typically by robust reds and blues. Another feature found in some pieces from this area is the practice of using thread made of cotton and wool twisted together for the white (see plates 67 and 68). Because the wool in the mixture invariably tends to an ivory colour with age, the white areas assume a pleasant stippled, almost textured "salt and pepper" effect.

Plate 63 (opposite) is a detail from a Malatya-Gaziantep kilim. The warm, rich tones of these old natural dyes work together splendidly in this unusual motif set against matted white cotton. Note the use of contour weft wrapping to outline and emphasise the design.

Plate 63

FLATWEAVES OF TURKEY ▨ 99

PLATE 64

ADANA – GAZIANTEP KILIM

Size: 197 x 123 cm.

Warp: Wool, S plied   53/10 cm.

Weft: Wool, Z spun; cotton is used for the white areas   240-340/10 cm.

Colours: Nine – bordeaux red (varying shades), blue, yellow, straw grey, green, pale green, mauve, olive brown, white (cotton).

Technique: Slit-tapestry with extra brocade motifs, plus contour weft wrapping around the motifs. The warp ends are braided into a net at both ends. Lines of two-colour twining decorate the kilim at each end.

Condition: Very good.

Special Notes: The cotton is very matted.

Plate 64 illustrates a kilim which is much more enigmatic. The colours suggest a southern provenance, but it could equally as well have been woven by a group of Turkic tribesmen from Aleppo region who later occupied areas around Sivrihisar. It is an old piece, but in perfect condition. The overall composition, quality of colours and skill of weaving are all of a very high standard. It possesses a much more limited range of colours than the other pieces we illustrate in this section. In terms of numbers both of warps and wefts, it is very finely woven. The side borders are very interesting and cleverly devised; they consist of simple, stalked hooks floating freely in the white surround. By viewing the borders from another perspective, one is aware of the reciprocating white ramshorn hooks which form inserts in the more dominant coloured motifs. The decorative end borders can also be seen as reciprocal hooks which form a white, wavy, Turkoman line, or puppet-like figures. This kilim uses the elibelinde motif in a manner different from other kilims, shown in earlier pages, which have this design. Altogether, it is a very beautiful piece and one of our favourites.

PLATE 65

GAZIANTEP-ALEPPO KILIM
Two-Piece

Size: 375 x 192 cm.

Warp: Wool, S plied   48/10 cm.

Weft: Wool, Z spun, mostly used singly but in some places two strands are inserted together; cotton is used for the white areas   260/10 cm.

Colours: Seventeen – blue, pale blue, deep red, tomato red, red, pale red, burnt ochre, yellow, mustard, straw, olive green, lilac, fawn, brown, olive brown, reddish brown, white (cotton).

Technique: Slit-tapestry with contour weft wrapping around many figures.

Condition: Fairly good – there is some damage.

Special Notes: The cotton is very felted. The many intermediate shades make describing the colours difficult.

What prompted the weaver of the large kilim shown here to use such a wealth of colour and in such wondrous combinations? Was she trying to create a cooling garden, an oasis, to contrast with her harsh environs? Or was she merely following the dictates of tradition? Sheer speculative questions, these, but what is self-evident is a beautiful and skilfully woven kilim. It incorporates a large selection of colours, with major and minor design elements combining to produce a harmonious unity. In the vine-like outer borders, as well as the narrow minor borders separating the panels of the main field, the weaver has played with the colours she has had to hand, but her sense of colour balance remains superb throughout.

PLATE 66

GAZIANTEP-ALEPPO KILIM

Size: 166 x 110 cm.

Warp: Wool, S plied   50/10 cm.

Weft: Wool, Z spun; two strands are used together; cotton for white areas   220/10 cm.

Colours: Ten – pale red, deep blue, pale blue, yellow, orange, olive green, light grey, dark brown, light brown, white (cotton).

Technique: Slit-tapestry with eccentric weft outlining. A few small extra brocade motifs decorate the field.

Condition: Some brown has been restored; otherwise in very good condition.

Illustrated is a kilim with some similarities to the piece previously described. Side and end borders are totally different, but the main field is divided in the same manner into panels separated by minor borders, and it uses the same motifs. Altogether a much smaller piece with fewer colours, it has, however, a similar range of hues. White cotton again features prominently and, like the former piece, it has become very matted with age.

PLATE 67

GAZIANTEP-ALEPPO KILIM
Two-Piece

Size: 330 x 166 cm.

Warp: Wool, S plied   52/10 cm.

Weft: Wool, with wool and cotton plied together for the white areas; S plied   180/10 cm.

Colours: Thirteen – blue, dark blue, pale blue, cochineal red paling to pink, salmon, pink, pale bluish green, straw yellow, orange-yellow, mauve, lilac, brown, white (wool plus cotton mixture).

Technique: Slit-tapestry with contour weft wrapping around the motifs.

Condition: Good – it has had some repair.

The kilim shown here is made resplendent through its use of harmonising colours, which have mellowed with age. There is sufficient variety in the minor motifs within the carefully drawn recurring figures occupying the field to dispel any sense of monotony. Like many kilims from this area, the wefting yarn is plied. The white areas throughout are a blend of wool and cotton.

PLATE 68

GAZIANTEP-ALEPPO KILIM
Two-Piece

Size: 323 x 158 cm.

Warp: Wool, S plied   55/10 cm.

Weft: Wool, S plied, with wool and cotton plied together for the white areas   220/10 cm.

Colours: Thirteen – cochineal red, bright red, maroon, dark blue, light blue, turquoise, light green, yellow, bright orange, yellow-orange, brown, fawn, white.

Technique: Slit-tapestry weave.

Condition: Good – it has had minor repairs.

There can be little doubt about the provenance of the kilim illustrated in this plate. The quality of the colours, the tightly woven nature of the textile, and the design elements all point to the Gaziantep-Aleppo region. The mixture of cotton and wool used for the white areas of design provides a further determining feature. Without the confinement of side borders, a rather unusual feature for kilims of this area, the figures in the main field seem to expand outwards freely. The main patterns may appear rather simple and repetitive, but what makes this kilim especially attractive is the wonderful interplay of colours the weaver has used in developing certain of the minor motifs. Even some of the rows of hooks have their bases and tips worked in different colours.

PLATE 69

GAZIANTEP-ALEPPO KILIM

Size: 157 x 96 cm.

Warp: Wool, S plied   47/10 cm.

Weft: Wool, S plied   220/10 cm.

Colours: Fourteen – bright red, brownish red, maroon, cochineal red, blue, light blue, greyish blue, two shades of mauve, yellow, green, orange, brown, white.

Technique: Slit-tapestry weave with contour weft wrapping around some figures.

Condition: Good – some brown has been replaced.

Small pieces from this region, like the one shown, are always rare and most appear to be very old. Border and field designs, the subtle shifts in colour, and reds with a cochineal basis, are all characteristic of the south. Perhaps the most unusual feature is the apricot background of the borders, instead of the more common white.

PLATE 70

GAZIANTEP-ALEPPO KILIM
Two-Piece

Size: 435 x 163 cm.

Warp: Wool, S plied   52/10 cm.

Weft: Wool, Z spun, but in some areas S plied; cotton is used in some white areas   240-320/10 cm.

Colours: Thirteen – blue, pale turquoise, dark red, crimson, carmine red, pale yellow, lime green, mauve-purple, brown, dark reddish brown, reddish orange, ivory, white (cotton).

Technique: Slit-tapestry weave with contour weft wrapping around figures in the outer border; some extra brocade motifs.

Condition: Excellent.

There is a group of kilims which has come to be called Rashwan in the trade. Usually large, two-piece kilims, they have a field comprised of three lozenge-shaped figures built up into joined medallions. The same model appears to have been used by diverse groups, both Turkic and Kurdish, in various parts of southern and central Turkey. This is very uncommon, because different tribal groups are usually fiercely independent and normally reject influences of other groups, keeping instead to their own traditional forms.

Of the three examples we show, that in plate 70 appears to be most southern in origin. In its colouration, especially, and also in its materials, it has many affinities with kilims from the Gaziantep-Aleppo region. It uses considerable amounts of cochineal red, and a light mauve-purple aptly referred to as milk aubergine. The latter colour is only found in early kilims. One colour is very unusual – from a distance it appears a very deep blue but, on closer examination, it is seen to be orange-based wool over-dyed with blue. The cotton in the white areas of design is very matted, which is also indicative of great age – the cotton is largely confined to emphasising the medallions, but small amounts are inserted here and there among the wool in the borders.

PLATE 73

REYHANLI KILIM
Two-Piece

Size: 378 x 155 cm.

Warp: Wool, S plied   61/10 cm.

Weft: Wool, S plied; cotton is used for the white areas   200-260/10 cm.

Colours: Thirteen – dark blue, light blue, cochineal red, madder red, green (variable), orange varying to reddish orange, maroon, reddish brown, dark brown, yellow, orange-brown, dark straw, white (cotton).

Technique: Slit-tapestry weave with contour weft wrapping around some figures.

Condition: Excellent.

Of the several kilims that we have seen with this pattern, this one is a very tightly woven example. The basic layout in these kilims remains fairly constant, including the general arrangement of the colours. Variations in individual pieces occur in the borders and some of the minor fill-in motifs.

Although this piece may lack the instant appeal of many of the other kilims shown in this book, with their spontaneity and strong tribal features, one can admire its precision and skilled weaving. The colours, individually, have a wonderful quality; together they combine to produce a very harmonious kilim. As it is a representative of a distinct type, we felt justified in including it here.

This kilim was woven by a group of the Reyhanli tribe which, as mentioned earlier, made seasonal migrations as far north as Sivas. Large single-piece kilims with many similarities in design to this one once used to be quite common in the Sivas area.

PLATE 74

ÇUVAL

Size: 106 x 87 cm.

Warp: Wool, mostly white; in some places brown and white twisted together; S plied   47/10 cm.

Weft: Wool, Z spun   180/10 cm in plain weave areas; two S plied strands are inserted together in the design areas; cotton is used for white.

Colours: Ten – blue, brick red, coral red, reddish orange, purplish brown, yellow, khaki green, greyish green, pale mauve, white (cotton).

Technique: Two panels of modified zili brocade (offset 2:2 floats) and stripes of plain weave in different colours; there is a row of additional brocade figures at each end.

Condition: Good.

Within the triangle formed approximately by the towns of Adana, Kayseri and Malatya, an area largely of high mountains and deep valleys, lives a medley of Turkic and Kurdish clans. It is from here that a confusing array of çuvals originates. Often simply designated Maraş in the trade, they are sometimes difficult to separate into Turkic or Kurdish pieces, let alone to narrow them down as belonging to a certain group. Thus one is left speculating that some have influences from Malatya-area weavings, or finds in others similarities to Taurus Yörük pieces, or to southern, Gaziantep ones. The numerous tribal groups were not, of course, confined to this triangle, but wandered freely in various directions on their seasonal trek. This has added to the later confusion about where, and by whom, different articles were made.

There are still large numbers of nomads who have their quarters within this triangle. Some quite sizeable encampments of black tents can be found in various parts and, during spring and autumn, when the nomads recommence their seasonal migration, one often meets the colourfully bedecked trains with their accompanying flocks.

Presented in the next few pages is a variety of çuvals from the region in question, giving some idea of the range of designs that can be found. This assortment is by no means an exhaustive selection of the numerous kinds of "Maraş" çuvals available. Even in our own collection we have several other examples.

PLATE 75

ADANA-TAURUS ÇUVAL

Size: 117 x 84 cm.

Warp: Pairs of S plied white wool warps alternate with pairs of S plied black goat-hair warps   42/10 cm.

Weft: Wool, Z spun   200/10 cm.

Colours: Twelve – blue, madder red, orange-red, orange-yellow, lime yellow, reddish brown, pale burgundy, golden brown, pink, pale grey, pale lilac, ivory.

Technique: Slit-tapestry weave with the remains of contour weft wrapping around some figures. Apparently, from what is left of the back, the wefting material used there was white cotton.

Condition: It has some minor damage.

Bearing in mind that çuvals represent the most traditional of weavings, with each clan proudly retaining its own particular design, one should be able to relate a certain piece to a particular tribal group. Unfortunately today, with the discontinuation of weaving traditions, this knowledge seems to be no longer available.

Of the çuvals illustrated, those shown in plates 75, 76 and 77 seem to be from the Taurus Mountains area north and west of Adana. The lightning-flash designs separating the main panels are quite common in çuvals from these parts. The çuval shown in this plate has a dynamic freedom of expression. This, together with the quaint usage of warps divided into alternating pairs of black goat hair and white wool, provides it with a distinctly rustic appearance.

PLATE 76
ADANA-TAURUS ÇUVAL

Size: 83 x 71 cm.

Warp: Wool, S plied   61/10 cm.

Weft: Wool, Z spun   260/10 cm in the plain weave areas; two strands are inserted together in brocaded areas; cotton is used for some white areas.

Colours: Twelve – blue, coral red, brick red, pale red, yellow, lime yellow, straw, salmon, mauve, brown, maroon, white (cotton).

Technique: Two panels of countered soumak brocade and two panels of modified zili brocade (offset 2:2 floats) are separated by bands of tapestry weave decorated with a compressed zigzag-flash design; a row of scattered brocade motifs is at one end.

Condition: Good.

Special Notes: The centre of one motif is delineated with metallic thread.

In contrast with the çuvals shown previously, that shown here is exquisitely refined and precise, a real gem of a weaving. Both warps and wefts are made of finely spun thread, enabling the weaver to include delicate details. The centipede-like motif found in one of the soumak bands is reminiscent of similar figures found in some old Ersari Turkoman rugs.

PLATE 77

ADANA-TAURUS ÇUVAL

Size: 113 x 81 cm.

Warp: Wool, S plied   61/10 cm.

Weft: Wool, Z spun   220-300/10 cm in the plain weave areas; two strands are inserted together in brocade areas; cotton is used for the white.

Colours: Eight – two reds, blue, green, aubergine, yellow, brown, white (cotton).

Technique: The design panels are mainly modified zili brocade (offset 2:2 floats) with some countered soumak, separated by bands of tapestry weave.

Condition: Very good.

The fresh and resplendent colours of the çuval illustrated in the accompanying plate belie its age. Colours and design combine here to produce a weaving which is harmonious and beautiful in all aspects.

There is a very obvious relationship between this piece and the çuval shown in plate 76, although the motifs they have in common have been treated in slightly different ways.

PLATE 78

ÇUVAL

Size: 150 x 119 cm.

Warp: Strong white wool, S plied   58/10 cm.

Weft: Z spun wool is used for the plain weave areas   240/10 cm; two strands of S plied wool are used for the design bands, cotton for the white areas.

Colours: Seven – pale red, blue, blue-green, maroon, brown, pale yellow, white (cotton).

Technique: Two bands of countered soumak brocade, plus plain weave stripes in different colours.

Condition: Good, except for a few small holes.

The importance of white cotton, used to make the tribal emblematic figures stand out, is amply illustrated in this çuval. The bold, hooked figures, carefully executed in soumak, are emphatic even from some distance. In contrast, the colours used to dye the woollen components of the design in this çuval are warm and have mellowed with age.

Other çuvals that we have seen of this particular type have the same sequence of colours in the plain woven bands. This again points to the strength of tradition, not only in the weaving of the major design elements, but in minor details as well.

PLATE 79

MARAŞ ÇUVAL
Opened Out

Size: 152 x 82 cm.

Warp: Wool, S plied   52/10 cm.

Weft: Wool, S plied is used for the design areas, unplied, Z spun, in the bands of plain weave; cotton is used for the white areas   220-280/10 cm.

Colours: Nine – two blues, bordeaux, orange, maroon, yellow, blue-black, blue-green, white (cotton).

Technique: There is one main panel, bordered by two narrow bands, of slit-tapestry weave. The back consists of narrow stripes of slit-tapestry weave separated by wider bands of plain weave. Fine lines of 1:1 zili, in black and white, edge these stripes. There are a few scattered extra brocade figures.

Condition: Good.

Shown here is a representative of a distinct genre of çuval. In the few examples we possess and the several others we have seen, the front panel design remains basically similar to this one, with minor variations. Where they do differ is in the way the colours are used and especially in the design of the minor bands. Often the backs of the bags, like this one, are also patterned and woven in resplendent colours. In the past, similar çuvals could occasionally be found around Cihanbeyli, 100 kilometres north of Konya. Long ago, part of a Kurdish tribe from the Maraş area settled in this region.

The Kurds are very much a forgotten people, receiving scant mention in many books on the Middle East and being completely overlooked in others. The Kurdish population numbers many millions. The greatest concentration is in eastern Turkey; there are slightly fewer in Iran, less again in Iraq, with the smallest segment in Syria.

For thousands of years they have been a very important force in those parts. During a period of more than a thousand years, starting about 4 000 years ago, Medes and Persians, both of Aryan stock, moved southwards in small groups from the Caucasus and the steppes north of the Caspian Sea. These Aryan people had a high level of culture and were better organised than the indigenous populations. In spite of being a minority they soon subjugated the region's existing inhabitants. Their progression towards the south and west was periodically interrupted by other groups moving out of Asia Minor, such as the Iberians, whom we now know as Georgians. The Armenians are another group who also may have come from the west. The invading groups usually slowly integrated with the original populations, so that none remained racially pure. It was from the Medes, who during those early times took possession of the mountainous areas in western Iran, that the present-day Kurds have arisen.

Throughout later history the territory occupied by the Kurds was often claimed by some larger neighbour, be it Achaemenid Persia, Assyria, Armenia, the Arabs, or others. However, the mountainous terrain was so inaccessible that many of the conquering forces preferred to bypass Kurdish lands. Though subjugated in name, the Kurds were often left much to themselves.

So what we now know as Kurds are a people stemming from a Medean branch of the Aryans, mixed with indigenous populations and diverse invaders. Consequently, their physical features and build vary in different regions according to the mixture with other peoples. One rebel leader in Iraq defined Kurds as those who feel they are Kurds. The name "Kurd" was originally bestowed on them by the Arabs, the people themselves in the past preferring to go under their various clan names. Today they all readily refer to themselves as Kurds.

Apart from their customs and the way they dress, they have, of course, one important bond in common – their language. There are three distinct dialects in Kurdish, all, like modern Persian, originating from the Pahlavi language of Sassanid Iran. The central one, named Kermanji, is used by more than 50 per cent of all Kurds.

In Turkey, two of the dialects are spoken; Kermanji south of Lake Van, and Zaza north of a line running approximately from Van to Diyarbakir. Zaza is also understood by Kermanji-speaking Kurds; in the area between Erzincan and Elazığ it is very much influenced by Turkish.

The Kurds in the high mountainous country have kept to themselves but in other parts they have integrated readily with Turks.

The precisely drawn motif in plate 80 (opposite), taken from an old çuval, is executed in wonderful glowing tones. The weaver has obviously enjoyed weaving this piece. Note the way she has interspersed different shades in some of the colours.

PLATE 80

PLATE 81

MALATYA-GAZIANTEP ÇUVAL

Size: 139 x 90 cm.

Warp: Mainly greyish brown goat hair; some warps are a mixture of wool and goat hair; S plied   56/10 cm.

Weft: Wool, unplied Z spun   220/10 cm in plain weave areas, S plied in design areas, plus metallic thread for highlights.

Colours: Eleven – dark blue, light blue, bordeaux red, brick red, green, brown, reddish orange, khaki, ivory, black, gold plus white (metallic).

Technique: Two bands of finely executed 2:1 pure soumak worked in one direction. The design wefts are carried back under the motifs creating an embossed effect because of the double thickness of the wefts. The remainder of the weaving is made up of stripes of plain weave in different colours.

Condition: It has sustained some damage.

The splendid colours used in this çuval have maintained their freshness and vibrancy despite the age of the piece. These are natural dyes at their best. A substantial amount of metallic thread has been used to highlight certain features of the design.

Like the heybes illustrated in plates 100 and 102, this çuval is woven with that rather rare type of soumak, worked in one direction only, that we describe in the section on techniques. Figure 9 shows a close-up detail of this method.

As with so many of the çuvals we have seen over the years, this piece has had a change of function. Judging from the damage it has sustained, it once must have been used for its original purpose, as a storage bag. Later generations, recognising its artistry and skilled weaving, have opened out the bag, turned over its ends, and displayed it as a decorative hanging.

PLATE 82

DIRICAN PRAYER KILIM

Size: 131 x 84 cm.

Warp: Wool, light pink, S plied   49/10 cm.

Weft: Wool, S plied   280/10 cm, and metallic thread (gold and cotton).

Colours: Seven – maroon-red, blue, dark blue, orange, straw yellow, mauve-brown, white (metallic).

Technique: Slit-tapestry with some contour weft wrapping.

Condition: Good.

Special Notes: Large amounts of metallic thread have been used in this kilim.

In the mountainous tracts which virtually surround Malatya, a small city in central eastern Turkey, are numerous villages. Some are populated by Turkic people, others by Kurds, and some by both. As far as we are able to ascertain, most of the old weavings originating from these parts were woven by Kurds, probably because this group of people has kept closer to its tribal roots than the settled agriculturists of Turkic origin.

Some of the weavings are very distinctive and can readily be identified as coming from a specific area in this region. Such a group are those from around Dirican, a small village south-east of Malatya. A particular mauve-red colour, with the tendency to mute to a paler mauve on exposure to light, is very typical of Dirican-area weavings.

Some old Dirican flatweaves possess a beautiful red hue as well. It is a pity that this colour was not more widely used. The kilims are invariably thin and finely woven. Metallic highlights are a common feature, as is a form of an eight-pointed star (see plates 82 and 84). Strangely, most of the kilims we have seen from this area are distorted, with one edge being longer than the other.

PLATE 83
DIRICAN KILIM

Size: 140 x 80 cm.

Warp: Wool, S plied   54/10 cm.

Weft: Wool, S plied   200/10 cm; also some metallic thread.

Colours: Eleven – dark red, light red, pale maroon-red, blue, light blue, yellow, blue-green, light reddish brown, chocolate brown, white (cotton), gold (metallic).

Technique: Slit-tapestry with contour weft wrapping around some of the designs. The warp ends are formed into a web and then plaited into tassels, tapered at their base.

Condition: Good.

Like the last kilim shown, this piece has features that are typical of the Dirican area. It has the same thin texture, achieved through the use of finely spun wool for both warps and wefts. Considerable amounts of metallic thread have also been included to highlight certain areas of design. Note also the distortion of the sides of the weaving.

The quality of the colours is, however, much richer and more vibrant than the former piece. Also evident is the contrast between the muted mauve and the deep bordeaux, where one batch of the dye has undergone change.

A comparison with plates 70, 71 and 72 will show that this kilim, although substantially smaller, is basically of the same design.

PLATE 84

PORĞA HEYBE

Size: 176 x 74 cm.

Warp: Wool, S plied   48/10 cm.

Weft: Wool, S plied in design areas   220-260/10 cm, unplied Z spun in plain weave areas   300/10 cm; cotton is used for white areas; there are considerable metallic highlights.

Colours: Twelve – two blues, red, bordeaux, blue-green, green, yellow, orange, mauve, dark brown, white (cotton), gold (metallic).

Technique: The face of the bag is executed in slit-tapestry technique, the back consists of narrow stripes of plain weave in blue and red; the warp ends at the mouth of the bag are braided together.

Condition: Good.

Bags with the quality of design and richness of colour of this one are rare. The weaver was able to accomplish the very precise and refined drawing of the figures through her choice of finely spun, superior-quality wool. The colours are very similar to those used for the kilim shown in plate 83, except all the bordeaux here has undergone the muting process. Besides metallic thread, cotton is also used to highlight some features.

This heybe comes from the region of a small village called Porğa, in the Dirican district. When discovered, it showed evidence of having been extensively used. Parts of it were very tattered and merely repaired with several generations of cloth patches. Although restoring it was a difficult and time-consuming task, it provided much pleasure because one could really appreciate the original skilful weaving and, at the same time, feast ones' eyes on the splendid colour combinations.

PLATE 85

DIRICAN YASTIK

Size: 95 x 49 cm.

Warp: Orange-brown wool, S plied   42/10 cm.

Weft: Wool, S plied on the face   220-240/10 cm, unplied Z spun on the back   220-240/10 cm, plus some gold metallic-thread highlights.

Colours: Eight – midnight blue, bright blue, brick red, mustard yellow, pale lime green, beige, gold (metallic), dark brown.

Technique: Slit-tapestry on the face, with a few scattered brocade motifs. The diagonal lines are executed in a multiple 2:2 weave (see also figs 14 and 15) and weft wrapped for emphasis. The back is woven in plain weft-faced weave in stripes of red and brown. A row of brocade S motifs adorns one stripe.

Condition: Very good.

From the condition of the yastik illustrated here it would appear to have had very little use. The contour weft wrapping and the scattered brocade figures are still very complete. Unusually, the last have been constructed using threads of two different colours.

Again, this piece has features that allow one to readily distinguish it as having been woven in the Dirican region, especially the range of colours that are employed. The red, however, has a warmer orange tone than the weavings that we have already discussed from this area. Like the preceding piece the quality of the colours is enhanced by the lustrous wool.

PLATE 86

ADIYAMAN CICIM BROCADE
Two-Piece

Size: 300 x 158 cm.

Warp: Wool, S plied   51/10 cm.

Weft: Wool, Z spun; ground weft   260-280/10 cm.

Colours: Eleven – blue, pale blue, turquoise, two reds, mauve, yellow, green, brown, orange-brown, ivory.

Technique: Solid design cicim alternating with bands of plain blue and red weave. Warp ends have been braided and plaited into tassels.

Condition: Very good.

Kurdish weavers are renowned for their use of subtle variations of intermediate shades of colour. A particularly striking example of this is seen in the large cicim brocade shown alongside. Probably woven in the Adiyaman area, to the south of Malatya, this is an excellent piece to illustrate how skilful the weavers could be in coordinating their palette of colours. Some of the shifts in shading are very delicate. Nothing clashes; instead there is total harmony. This large weaving is tightly woven and must have demanded a great amount of time and patience of the weaver. Considerable care has been put into its finish – the selvedges are carefully overbound with threads of different colours, and at each end the warps are first tightly braided into a sturdy band and then bundled together to form knotted tassels.

PLATE 87

ZILI BROCADE HEYBE

Size: 198 x 103 cm.

Warp: Wool, S plied   61/10 cm.

Weft: Wool, S plied for brocade, unplied Z spun in plain weave areas   240-260/10 cm.

Colours: Eight – two blues, madder, rust red, reddish orange, aubergine, dark brown, ivory.

Technique: The bag faces are worked in design-filling offset 3:3 zili; the back is plain weft-faced weave in stripes of different colours; two brocade motifs (almost like monograms) adorn the back of one of the bags.

Condition: Very good, except for one small hole.

Compared with the cicim in plate 86, the use of colour in the zili heybe shown here is much sparser, but it is beautiful in its own way. The product of an obviously skilled and very experienced weaver, its design is carefully controlled throughout. It is so tightly woven that individual warps have become raised during the beating down of the wefts, resulting in a corded effect.

PLATE 88

MALATYA-SIVAS PRAYER KILIM

Size: 169 x 95 cm.

Warp: Wool, S plied   52/10 cm.

Weft: Wool, Z spun; cotton is used in the white areas   180-300/10 cm; also some metallic thread.

Colours: Ten – blue, bright red, cochineal red, brick red, orange, maroon, yellow, green (variable from turquoise to olive green), dark brown, white (cotton).

Technique: Slit-tapestry with some extra brocade figures; remains of some contour weft wrapping. At one end the warps are plaited into tassels.

Condition: It is considerably damaged.

In spite of the damage that this prayer kilim has sustained over its many generations of existence, it has retained a freshness and vitality of colour. It embodies all the qualities of Kurdish weaves at their best, exemplified in the lustrous, tightly spun wool, the care given to its design and, above all, its harmony of colour. As with so many old pieces, the cotton used for the white areas has become very matted.

In a village some distance from Malatya, we were told it was the practice in the past for the women to ask the Ağa, the local chief, for selected parts of fleeces in return for their labour of shearing the sheep. This probably accounts for the superb quality of wool found in many older kilims and other flatweaves from this area.

PLATE 89

HAKKARI HEYBE

Size: 153 x 80 cm.

Warp: Wool, S plied   65/10 cm.

Weft: Wool, S plied for brocade of bag faces, unplied Z spun for the back   200/10 cm.

Colours: Thirteen – blue, red, yellow, maroon, pale blue-green, dark brown, chocolate brown, olive brown, ivory, small amount of bright orange; in addition, the binding of the side cords contains pink, burnt orange, khaki green.

Technique: The bag faces are worked in modified zili brocade (offset 2:2 floats); the back consists of stripes of weft-faced weave in different colours. The sides are bound with different colours, ending in a tuft of wool at each corner.

Condition: Very good.

The far south-eastern part of Turkey, east of Siirt, consists of high mountain ranges, with some areas being virtually inaccessible. The climate is harsh and in many parts snow covers the villages for the greater part of the year. For more than 3 000 years Kurds have controlled these mountain heights. Unsurpassed guerilla fighters, they have successfully defended their inhospitable terrain from invaders through the ages and have never been entirely subjugated.

Throughout their history they have had no interest in establishing a political entity, but have preferred to live a semi-nomadic existence in tribal groups, often feuding with neighbouring clans. Keen plunderers, they usually took the chance to form looting parties during periods of political unrest, raiding villages and even cities in western Azerbaijan.

Richard Burton, in a footnote to his translation of *The Book of the Thousand Nights and a Night,* writes of them:

> The Kurds are of a Persian race, speaking an old barbarous Iranian tongue. They are born bandits, highwaymen and cattle lifters, yet they have spread extensively over Syria and Egypt and produced some glorious men, witness Sultan Salah al Din (Saladin) the Great.

PLATE 90

SIIRT KILIM WITH CICIM BROCADE

Size: 205 x 113 cm.

Warp: Brown wool, S plied   38/10 cm.

Weft: Wool and goat hair, Z spun in plain weave areas   160-260/10 cm; S plied wool and some cotton is used for brocade areas.

Colours: Seven – madder red, dark brown, black (goat hair), blue, bordeaux, salmon, white (cotton).

Technique: Bands of design-filled cicim, separated by bands of plain weave in different colours containing scattered cicim motifs. There are selvedges in different colours over four pairs of warps on either side. The warp ends are braided into thick straps at each end.

Condition: Good – it has had some repair.

Although officially the population of Turkey is one, modern-day Kurds of the south-east are still, for a large part, fiercely tribal in make-up and they adhere to their old way of life. The individual tribes were mostly under the leadership of chieftains, although at times they temporarily formed confederations. Only in recent times have nationalistic aspirations been entertained, a movement which is associated with the new class of Kurdish intellectuals. Many of these educated Kurds studied abroad, where they came under the influence of foreign political and social doctrines. In Iraq the Kurds have been striving for freedom and over the last decades, on several occasions, they have fought prolonged battles with government forces.

Chief among the attributes of the Kurds of these regions are personal courage and an absolute loyalty to their tribal group. A favourite winter pastime is smuggling. The high mountain ranges in the border countries are, in winter, exceptionally forbidding. Government patrols are no match for the hardy Kurds, whose guile and prowess in traversing the mountain passes are born of their long experience in the area.

In the mountains in the region of Siirt we have found a few examples of three different kinds of brocade weavings not seen elsewhere. Two types are illustrated in plates 90 and 91.

PLATE 91

SIIRT KILIM WITH CICIM BROCADE

Size: 270 x 134 cm.

Warp: Strong, ivory-coloured wool, S plied   37/10 cm.

Weft: Wool, Z spun in the plain weave areas 240-260/10 cm; S plied wool is used for the brocade motifs.

Colours: Nine – bright madder red, orange-red, navy blue, dark greyish blue, midnight blue, dark brown, fawn, camel, ivory.

Technique: The weaving consists of bands of cicim alternating with bands of plain weave in various colours. Along one edge is a column of zigzag cicim motifs; on the other are a few chevrons worked in cicim. On each side is a selvedge in zones of red and blue over four pairs of warps. The warp ends are braided at each end and were once plaited into tassels, a few of which remain.

Condition: Generally good – it has some slight areas of damage.

The ivory ground pieces, like the one illustrated, are generally larger than the mainly red background type shown in plate 90. The third class of cicim, the smallest in size, is elaborately brocaded with an all-over pattern done mainly in orange and rose red, or soft pinks, and some blue.

These brocades are always woven in one piece, using tightly spun, strong and glossy wool. The wefts are beaten down firmly, resulting in a ribbed texture. Note the zigzag patterns executed in red and blue along one side of the piece illustrated here – this appears to be a typical feature, since the other cicim brocades we have seen of this type all carry this peculiarity.

PLATE 92

SIIRT KILIM
Two-Piece

Size: 327 x 132 cm.

Warp: Goat hair, S plied, one strand of fawn together with one dark brown   42/10 cm.

Weft: Wool and goat hair, S plied   140-320/10 cm.

Colours: Eight – blue, midnight blue (goat hair), red, maroon, orange, greyish yellow, yellow, ivory.

Technique: Slit-tapestry kilim. The warp ends are braided together to form a thick band. The remains of selvedges in a variety of colours over three pairs of warps on each side can be seen in places.

Condition: Good.

Shown is a Kurdish kilim which, from its material and weave, we can attribute to the area southwest of Lake Van. As with the piece in Plate 90, the dark blue, almost black areas of the wefting consist of finely spun goat hair, and the method of finishing the selvedges is the same. The warps of this kilim are made of coarse goat hair that has been tightly spun into a fine thread – a difficult task with such intractable fibre. It must be the work of a very accomplished spinner. The colours are few, but used tastefully. From the quality of the colours it appears that this kilim was woven early last century.

urther east the mountains are very high and hard to penetrate. The so-called Van-Hakkari kilims of this south-eastern region are often easy to recognise. While the separation of the various tribal groups by mountains has contributed to a diversity of designs, a few basic characteristics can be discerned. Their shape and size is fairly constant. Occasionally they are woven in one piece but more usually in two halves. The warps are generally thick, made of strong wool or goat hair; the warp ends are almost always braided into a thick web and then every ten to twenty plaited into heavy tassels. The wefts are of fine, lustrous, plied wool of excellent quality, tightly packed down so a ribbed effect is produced as they pass over and under the much heavier warps. For small ornamentations, gold or silver metallic thread was often used.

Perhaps because of their long association with a particular environment and the dye plants growing there, the Kurds were renowned for the dyes that they obtained. Although often lacking a great range of colour, their skill lay in producing subtle intermediate shades. The weavers from this area used a palette consisting mainly of shades of blue, red, a brown that varies from pale to almost black, white, blue-green, and a shade that ranges from sunflower yellow via a beautiful deep orange to light red. The balanced use of these natural colours in older kilims certainly demonstrates the artistry of the weavers at their best. Old, plant-dyed Van-Hakkari kilims are now extremely rare.

Plate 93 (opposite) is a detail of plate 94. Note the precision of detail achieved by a skilled weaver using tightly spun wool of excellent quality. Some of the small, central, whitish ornaments are woven using metallic thread.

PLATE 93

PLATE 94

HAKKARI-KAŞURAN KILIM
Two-Piece

Size: 232 x 166 cm.

Warp: Strong olive brown and greyish brown wool S plied   50/10 cm.

Weft: Wool, mostly S plied, some unplied Z spun in the more open field areas   240-340/10 cm; highlights in metallic thread; in one half some of the white is cotton.

Colours: Eleven – orange-red, bordeaux, blue, navy blue, deep greenish blue, brownish mauve, reddish brown, dark walnut brown, yellow (sparingly used), ivory, white with gold (metallic).

Technique: Slit-tapestry with weft-wrapping around many figures. The various components in the large bands of design are separated by lines of soumak which run across the kilim.

Condition: Good, except for one end which is slightly frayed.

The Kaşuran kilim illustrated here is woven with the technical skill and artistry found only in some old weavings produced by this Kurdish group. All aspects of this kilim are superb – the quality of the wool, the spinning, colours and weave. Such kilims reflect the aristocracy of spirit that these fierce and proud tribesmen sustained. Anyone who has had the privilege of meeting these mountain people of south-east Turkey cannot but be impressed by their resolute strength of character.

PLATE 95

HAKKARI-KAŞURAN KILIM
Two-Piece

Size: 219 x 142 cm.

Warp: Brown, white and orange dyed wool and goat hair, S plied   35/10 cm.

Weft: Wool, Z spun, majority unplied, some plied 160-200/10 cm.

Colours: Eleven – blue, midnight blue, coral red, pinkish red, orange, pale orange, orange-yellow, brown, khaki brown, deep maroon, ivory.

Technique: Slit-tapestry with contour weft wrapping and soumak lines. The warp ends are braided and plaited into tassels and tied with coloured wool.

Condition: Very good.

This kilim is one of the most beautiful pieces that we have seen from this region and is in excellent condition. Although there are numerous inconsistencies, the total effect is both harmonious and pleasing. The shades of the various colours change throughout the kilim; in spite of its age, they have kept their freshness and beauty. There is also some variation in the ornamentation. Note, for example, that the end borders are totally different. As we have noted earlier, one of the characteristics of kilims from the eastern region is that the surface has a pronounced ribbed effect resulting from the use of thick warps. This feature is pronounced here. The warps of this piece are made of wool and goat hair of different colours. Even the plaiting and cording of the warp ends contribute to its appeal.

PLATE 96

HAKKARI KILIM
Two-Piece

Size: 236 x 183 cm.

Warp: Wool, S plied, mainly greyish brown, with one band of light brown 32/10 cm.

Weft: Wool, S plied 170/10 cm.

Colours: Ten – blue, blue-green, madder red, orange-red, reddish orange, orange, light orange, yellow, dark brown, ivory.

Technique: Slit-tapestry weave. The warp ends are braided into a narrow band and then groups of them are plaited into stout tassels; pairs of tassels are subsequently tied together with coloured thread.

Condition: Good.

Here is a kilim with a totally different concept of colour and design. The composition of this piece, with its six columns of figures, is unusual. Normally, kilims with this type of pattern possess only five columns, so that the halves are woven unequal in width, one half bearing three columns, the other two. The kilim further differs from the usual arrangement of the design in that the figures are turned 90 degrees and each is a composite unit, instead of being broken up, as seems customary. The effect is to provide a less crowded field than other kilims that we have seen of this type. The motifs of this piece appear to be more archetypal. Note the birdlike figures in the corners of each. The gradation of colour from a pale orange through to a rich red is very attractive, complemented as it is by the lustre of the wool.

PLATE 97

HAKKARI-HERKI KILIM

Size: 254 x 152 cm.

Warp: White wool and brown goat-hair mixture, S plied   33/10 cm.

Weft: Wool, S plied, design bands 240/10 cm; plain bands   100/10 cm.

Colours: Eleven – blue, light blue, turquoise, brick red, mauve, pale lilac, yellow, orange, dark brown, straw, ivory.

Technique: Bands of slit-tapestry alternating with cruder plain weave; contour weft wrapping around many motifs; numerous brocade motifs.

Condition: Good.

The harsh climate in the mountainous region south-east of Van encourages weavers to produce sturdy and tightly woven textiles. This is particularly evident in the kilim alongside. The thick warps are spun from a mixture of white and brown goat hair. An interesting feature of this piece is that the panels of design and the borders are woven using finely spun wefts, whereas the wefting of the intermediate areas of the field is very thick. This contrast in thickness gives a varied texture and adds to the vigour of the composition.

PLATE 98

HAKKARI-HERKI SOUMAK BROCADE
Two-Piece

Size: 237 x 150 cm.

Warp: Wool, dyed light purplish red, S plied   41/10 cm.

Weft: Wool, S plied for the brocade areas and much of the plain weave, except for some deep red and orange-red which is unplied   170-180/10 cm.

Colours: Eight – blue, light blue, dark blue, blue-green, deep red, orange-red, orange, ivory.

Technique: Bands of 2:1 soumak brocade, separated by bands of tapestry weave with alternating lightning-flash motifs and plain stripes. At one end the fabric is turned over and bound; at the other the warps are plaited into flat, tapered tassels.

Condition: Good, except for one small hole.

The Herki tribe is famous for its various textiles. Large parts of the tribe live in the mountains of the Tergever and Mergever districts near the border of Turkey, west and south-west of the Iranian town of Rezaiyeh. Other sections live in Hakkari Province of Turkey, and north-west of Irbil in Iraq. In the turbulent history of the past 150 years or so, the Herki tribesmen featured prominently as astute fighters, always ready to join any war party where there was a prospect of loot.

The women made beautiful kilims and soumak brocades, often highlighted with areas of silk. However, with the introduction of synthetic dyes, the products, though technically still well made, began to include very gaudy colours.

Only a few shades of red, two of blue and a blue-green form the prevailing colours of the old brocade weaving in plate 98. The subtly applied and rather sombre main colours are relieved here and there by the bright secondary colours used in the small ornamentations. The structure of the rug is almost stiff because of the wefts which are firmly beaten down. It is interesting to note that its colour scheme has close affinities with the Siirt in plate 90 and some of the textiles of the Yüncü Yörüks. It was, indeed, an unexpected surprise to discover this Herki in a shop among some very indifferent Hakkari kilims.

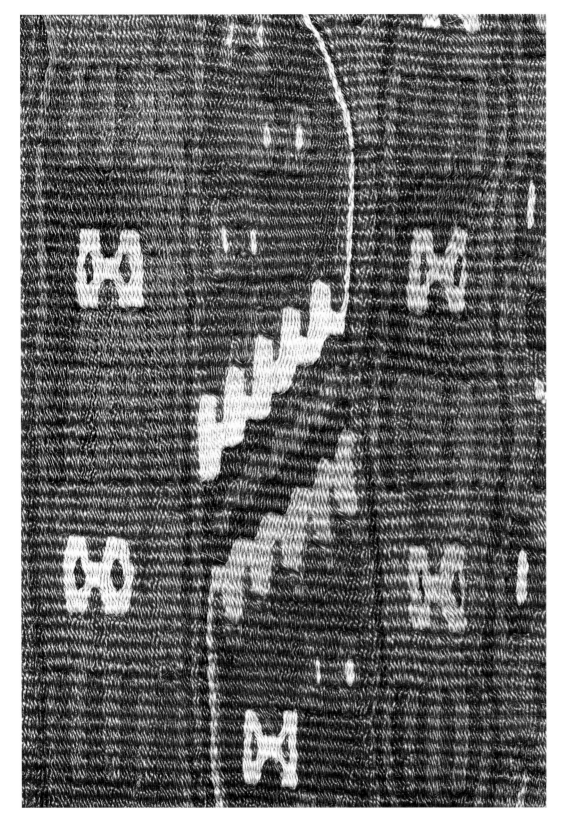

PLATE 99

DETAIL OF EAST ANATOLIAN KILIM

Size: 276 x 137 cm.

Warp: Strong, dark brown wool, S plied   30/10 cm.

Weft: Wool, S plied   200-240/10 cm.

Colours: Eight – mauve-red, orange-red, dark blue, greenish blue, turquoise, yellow, pale orange, white.

Technique: Slit-tapestry kilim weave with the wefts applied eccentrically in many places; some figures are outlined with contour weft wrapping, others with extra eccentric wefts; wavy lines of soumak executed in mostly three or sometimes two colours separate some design panels.

Condition: Good.

With its austere, even somewhat sombre colouration, the kilim of which a close-up detail is shown here is, at first sight, easily overlooked. It is only on closer examination that one is made aware of how subtly the weaver has used her palette. The two shades of blue and the turquoise and the two shades of red are made to interact in a delightful way. The weaving itself is very accomplished. The finely spun thread has a glossy sheen and is tightly packed down to produce a firm and heavy textile. It is one of those pieces which continues to catch one's attention the more one looks at it. Far from having a boring and repetitive design, it is a lively weaving with numerous innovations.

From the nature of its wools and weaving, this kilim could well have been made by Herki people.

PLATE 100

EAST TURKEY HEYBE

Size: 163 x 88 cm.

Warp: Brown wool, S plied   40/10 cm.

Weft: Wool, S plied for the design areas, unplied Z spun in plain weave areas   180-240/10 cm.

Colours: Nine – blue, greenish blue, red, orange-red, bordeaux, reddish brown, dark brown, walnut brown, ivory.

Technique: The faces consist of bands of pure soumak, worked in one direction only, so that the double thickness of wefts as they are carried back under the figures gives an embossed effect. Some of the motifs are weft-wrapped. Between the soumak bands are stripes of plain weft-faced weave. The back is woven in stripes of plain weft-faced weave in various colours.

Condition: Good.

Special Notes: At the mouths of the bags a row of countered two-colour twining, worked with multistranded wool, is carried inside at intervals to create the loops for fastening the bags together. The sides are bound with wools of various colours.

It is very difficult to give the exact provenance of the weavings that came out of the regions east and north of Lake Van. Great demographic change has taken place in this area. Before the turn of the century, there had already been clashes between Armenians and Kurds.

Up to the time of World War I the population of the disputed area consisted of about one-third Armenians, but the bulk of the peoples north of the line running approximately through Ağri to Iğdir, just to the north of Mount Ararat, were Turks and a small number of other groups. The people south of this line were mainly Kurds.

In the period leading up to World War I the Armenian nationalists came to believe that the Russians would help them create an independent Armenia in eastern Turkey. In 1914 the Armenians allied themselves with Russia against Turkey, while the Kurds sided with Turkey. Armenian volunteers formed battalions and invaded Turkey, together with the Russian armies. As a result of these clashes, the death toll on both sides was horrendous. It is estimated that more than 600 000 Kurds were killed. In retaliation, Turkey, during 1915 and 1916, deported more than 700 000 Armenians to Syria and Iraq, then still part of the Ottoman Empire. Few survived; most of the Armenians were robbed and killed by Kurds and Arabs, or died of starvation en route. By the end of the war, only a fraction of the original population of the eastern provinces of Turkey was left.

The Kurds have since moved into the empty spaces vacated by the Armenians and have gradually expanded further northwards to Kars. In Erzerum, also, they now form a large part of the population. The turmoil that affected these regions during the later part of last century and early this century explains why it is difficult to attribute old kilims from the eastern provinces to any definite group.

There is a great variety of designs in the kilims of these regions, but they share many features in common. Their colouration is distinct, consisting of deep and varied tints. Their thick warps are made of soft brown wool, frequently of two shades plied together; the warp ends are customarily braided into a thick band at either end. Outlining of design elements with extra wefts, so typical of kilims from most weaving areas in Anatolia, is rarely done here. The wefts are usually very fine and tightly plied, and, on older kilims, possess considerable lustre, but the weave is less dense than that found in Van-Hakkari kilims further south. A further distinction is that the kilims, even very large ones, are woven in one piece.

PLATE 101

KAĞIZMAN KILIM
Dated 1253 = 1837

Size: 223 x 158 cm.

Warp: Dark brown wool, S plied 36/10 cm.

Weft: Wool, S plied 160-220/10 cm.

Colours: Twelve – coral red, cochineal red, brownish blue, bright blue, light blue, yellow, straw, turquoise, pale lilac, brown, reddish brown, ivory.

Technique: Slit-tapestry weave.

Condition: Good – the fringes have been replaced.

The composition of this kilim has a certain simple naivety. The colours, however, are rich and possess that quality which is only to be seen in old weavings.

Note the hominoid figures in the end borders. These are frequently found in kilims from this area (see also, for example, plates 105 and 107).

PLATE 102

EAST TURKEY HEYBE

Size: (of design area): 83 x 83 cm.

Warp: Light brown and fawn wool, S plied   47/10 cm.

Weft: Wool, S plied in the design areas 200-220/10 cm; in the plain weave areas 240-260/10 cm.

Colours: Twelve – rust red, wine red, pale mauve, navy blue, blue, greyish blue, blue-green, yellow, light salmon, reddish brown, walnut brown, ivory.

Technique: The design panels consist of bands of pure soumak worked in one direction only, separated by narrow stripes of plain weave. Some of the figures are weft-wrapped. The back of the heybe is made up of narrow bands of plain weave in different colours.

Condition: One panel is very good, the other one reasonable.

Special Notes: An exceptionally old and fine piece, with lustrous wool.

The heybe illustrated here is woven using the same pure soumak technique as that in plate 100. (See also fig. 9.) Likewise, the wool is highly lustrous and finely spun. The colours used here are wonderfully subtle and suggest that this piece is indeed very old. Note the effective use of extra weft outlining, worked in a golden colour, around the figures in the central panel. This heybe used to have tufts of coloured silk inserted in rows between the design panels, but these have been largely chafed away.

PLATE 103

KAĞIZMAN KILIM
Fragment

Size: 157 x 75 cm.

Warp: Brown wool, S plied   31/10 cm.

Weft: Wool, S plied   280/10 cm.

Colours: Ten – red, orange, blue, deep turquoise, cochineal red, brown, maroon, khaki yellow, bluish green, white.

Technique: Slit-tapestry weave.

Condition: Good.

This appears to be an entire kilim but is undoubtedly a fragment. There is much to enjoy in this piece, from the quality of its wool and colours to the skilful way the design elements build up the pattern. The central panel is particularly noteworthy in this respect, its entire composition being an involved arrangement of small crosses.

PLATE 104
KAĞIZMAN KILIM

Size: 270 x 168 cm.

Warp: Light brown wool, S plied   48/10 cm.

Weft: Wool, mostly plied, some unplied Z spun 200-240/10 cm.

Colours: Thirteen – blue, blackish blue, blue-green, two reds, mauve-purple, terracotta, orange-yellow, straw yellow, chocolate brown, dark brown, khaki green, ivory.

Technique: Slit-tapestry weave. The warp ends are braided.

Condition: Good.

So-called Kars–Kağizman kilims at first glance often appear rather sombre, but closer inspection reveals a delicate harmony of colours, often with a tremendous variety of hues. While such pieces are mostly referred to as either Kars or Kağizman – although the name Kağizman seems to have ascendancy for the types of kilims we show here – it must be realised that these names are purely convenient and probably quite inaccurate. The tendency to bundle diverse weavings under one name is attractive because it is so tidy, but it can lead to a thoroughly false impression of where, and by whom, they were made.

Like the kilim in plate 101, the kilim illustrated here possesses all the features of eastern weavings. Although their designs are quite different, these two kilims are closely related in structure and colouration. This piece is altogether finer and has tremendous gradation of colour and a multitude of detail. Many aspects of this kilim suggest that it is older than the dated one.

PLATE 105

KAĞIZMAN KILIM

Size: 363 x 167 cm.

Warp: Brown wool, S plied   36/10 cm.

Weft: Wool, S plied   240/10 cm.

Colours: Thirteen – blue, turquoise, brick red, brownish red, orange-red, Prussian blue, lime yellow, straw, yellow-orange, cochineal red, dark brown, mauve, ivory.

Technique: Slit-tapestry weave. Warp ends are plaited into a continuous band.

Condition: Good.

Special Notes: A reed lattice screen in the Fine Arts Museum of San Francisco shows similarities in design. (See also *Hali* magazine, No. 25.)

The large kilim in plate 105 is very intricately designed. One cannot help being filled with admiration and respect for the woman who, using a simple spindle, spun the wool so finely, then dyed the yarn with such varied and beautiful natural colours to create, without recourse to a cartoon, such a harmonious piece of art. The design used was probably kept within the clan and passed down from generation to generation. How clearly must the total composition, together with all minor details, be stored in the woman's head for her to weave a piece like this with such perfection! Note how precisely and strongly each of the yellow hooked figures in the centre of the three medallions is drawn. Altogether, it is really an amazing piece of work which will never be repeated now that the identities of the various tribes are fast disintegrating in our rapidly changing world.

As has happened with several pieces in our collection, it was sheer chance that led to the discovery of this one. A Kurdish dealer in Istanbul whom we know well goes every day to the *hammam* (Turkish bath). One day his masseur, also a Kurd, who escaped with the surviving members of his family from the massacres of the 1914-1918 period in eastern Turkey, mentioned that he had stored in a cupboard at his home a kilim that his grandmother had given him many years before. The dealer was invited to the masseur's home and bought the kilim from him. One of the authors was in the dealer's small shop when he returned, saw the kilim, took an instant liking to it and promptly procured it from him.

This dealer, by the name of Mehmed, had, while still a small child, fled with his mother and grandmother from eastern Turkey to Konya after his grandfather was killed by Armenian troops. Since early childhood he sought a living in Istanbul, starting off as a shoeshine boy and progressing to become the owner of his own carpet and kilim shop.

A couple of years ago Mehmed decided to visit relatives in the mountains of his native lands. He stayed with an uncle, who one day asked him to fetch a horse from a distant valley. Being the complete city slicker, Mehmed had no idea how to catch the horse, let alone harness it. He had to ask the assistance of a twelve-year-old boy.

When his uncle heard about Mehmed's failure in capturing the horse he was furious. He called his wife and, babe in arms, she was made to mount the horse and ride it round and round. Then the uncle threw a rifle to his wife, tossed a bottle some distance away and instructed his wife to shoot it. Without faltering in stride, the wife shot the bottle from the back of the moving horse.

The uncle spat at Mehmed's feet. "And she is only a woman! What on earth are you!" he uttered vehemently, but in less decent terms. Mehmed fled the presence of so much barbarity and vowed never to return to his homeland.

PLATE 106
EAST TURKEY ÇUVAL

Size: 127 x 82 cm.

Warp: Wool, S plied   58/10 cm.

Weft: Wool, S plied   180/10 cm in the design areas and
Z spun in the plain areas   180-190/10 cm; the bands of
golden brown are very fine   360/10 cm.

Colours: Seven – red, pinkish red, two shades of blue,
golden brown, grey-brown, ivory.

Technique: Three main panels of modified zili brocade
(offset 2:2 floats) separated by bands of plain weave
containing cicim motifs. Each brocade panel has lines of
soumak separating the bands of different design.

Damaged as it is, the çuval shown here is still
able to provide considerable enjoyment. Employing a simplicity of colouration and a design
composed on a single theme, it nevertheless has
an effective completeness and unity. The secret
probably lies in the superior wool used and the
skilful weaving. This is just one of the many
çuvals that use a modified zili technique often
wrongly referred to as offset reverse soumak.
The brocade panels are in remarkably good
condition compared with the remainder of the
bag, which goes to prove how strong brocading
can be. This feature, where the brocading has
remained virtually intact but plain woven areas
have worn badly, we have noticed in other
çuvals.

PLATE 107

KARS-ERZERUM KILIM

Size: 340 x 136 cm.

Warp: Cotton, S plied (eight strands) 55/10 cm.

Weft: Wool, S plied 240-280/10 cm.

Colours: Nine – blue, sea blue, red (paler towards one end), olive brown, dark brown, yellow-orange, maroon, pale green, ivory.

Technique: Slit-tapestry weave. The warp ends are braided at one end.

Condition: Good.

The warps of this kilim are made of finely spun cotton, an unusual feature for east Turkey weavings. This has resulted in a very thin textile which, although large, is quite light in weight. The question of who made this early 19th-century piece poses a dilemma. The guard stripes on either side of each main border are also to be seen in plates 104 and 108, while the main borders utilise designs similar to those found in plates 101 and 105, but with a greater precision of detail. The large archaic motifs, alternately coloured red and white, occupying the central field are strongly drawn. Their derivation is anyone's guess. They have slight similarities to the carnation motifs found in early Ottoman rugs and some later kilims from various parts of Anatolia, but it is more likely that this is an ancient and traditional configuration, whose origin centuries ago may have been a stylised animal form. This piece is a rare and fascinating, as well as noble, work of art, with a superb technical finish.

PLATE 108

KARS-KAĞIZMAN KILIM

Size: 350 x 160 cm.

Warp: Wool, S plied, a brown and a white strand twisted together   38/10 cm.

Weft: Wool, S plied   200/10 cm.

Colours: Fifteen – blue (dark to light), red, pale red, orange-red, cochineal red, straw yellow, pale green, orange, maroon, reddish brown, chocolate brown, dark brown, turquoise, pale lavender, ivory.

Technique: Slit-tapestry weave.

Condition: Good – small amounts of repair have been carried out.

Plate 108 illustrates a kilim with strong Caucasian design elements. This composition is not uncommon and was used well into the times of synthetic dyes, but the later pieces tend to have more murky colours with a partiality for an insipid pink. This piece probably dates from about the middle of last century, or even earlier. The wool has taken on a lovely sheen with age. The weaver has used many colours, almost all of which range in shade from dark to light, presenting a harmonious effect. Although the long axis of the kilim is obviously off centre, this has not worried the weaver. She has simply adjusted the width of the borders, added a series of small motifs to the wider side, and squashed up the field figures on the other. It is an interesting piece, with many improvisations, and so very different in all respects to the aristocratic kilim discussed previously.

The landscape of the north-east, away from the Black Sea, is mostly bleak and forbidding, and quite mountainous. The diversity of the population groups living here is reflected in the kilims they once produced. Despite their variety, usually they can be recognised by a combination of factors, such as the quality and twist of the wool used for warps and wefts, the weaving characteristics, the colours, and the basic design elements of their composition. The outlining of figures using additional wefts, practised elsewhere, is generally lacking in the kilims from north-eastern Anatolia, as it is also from those previously discussed, further to the south-east.

Kurdish influences, which are so prominent in eastern regions, are less pronounced here. Prayer kilims from this region are particularly splendid. Their high artistic level is matched by the technical skill with which they are woven, and is surely indicative of a long period of development that must have preceded the weaving of the extant pieces. Old kilims with natural dyes are becoming increasingly hard to find. The prices demanded for them are prohibitive for the ordinary collector.

The exact provenance of many of these kilims is now difficult to state with any degree of certainty. Many are lumped together under the name Erzerum. Some expert dealers from Istanbul and elsewhere will call one type Bayburt, while others will refer to the same group as Kağizman. A few have totally different ideas, with some books going to the extent of dividing them into Sivas, Bayburt or Erzerum according to the ground colour of their main borders. We believe that determining their location is not so simplistic and, until further field studies enable researchers to ascribe them more exactly, it is preferable to place them in the broader category of north-eastern.

However, it may be already too late to learn more about their origins, for in the past hundred years or so, these regions have seen several wars, upheavals and massacres, resulting in drastic changes in the population structure. All that can be stated with any assuredness is that the kilims in this grouping were made in scores of villages ranging from Kars and Kağizman to Erzerum, further west to Bayburt and Sivas, and possibly as far west as Tokat or even Çankiri.

Plate 109 (below) shows a detail from a çuval from north-eastern Turkey probably woven early last century. The motif is very interesting, with its somewhat irregular drawing. It is presented in an assortment of wonderful colours, which have kept their clarity despite their age.

PLATE 109

PLATE 110

NORTH-EAST TURKEY PRAYER KILIM

Size: 193 x 125 cm.

Warp: Wool, mostly one light brown plus one white strand twisted together, remainder all white, S plied 33/10 cm.

Weft: Wool, S plied 160-220/10 cm.

Colours: Ten – blue, two reds, orange, straw, yellow, brown, pale lilac, greyish white, ivory.

Technique: Slit-tapestry weave.

Condition: Good.

From the quality of its wool, its colour and its design, we consider the prayer kilim reproduced here to have been woven further eastwards towards Kars than the other pieces illustrated in this group. It has a heavier weave than the others, and some of the design elements are very reminiscent of Kars-area kilims. The range of hues has many similarities to the kilim which appears in plate 108.

PLATE 111

NORTH-EAST TURKEY PRAYER KILIM

Size: 195 x 149 cm.

Warp: Wool, S plied   39/10 cm.

Weft: Wool, cotton for white areas, S plied   180/10 cm.

Colours: Nine – blue, light blue, greenish blue, red (paler at one end), straw yellow, mauve, reddish brown, ivory, white (cotton).

Technique: Slit-tapestry weave.

Condition: Good – both sides have been restored.

Both in its design and its colours the kilim alongside is exceptional. The organisation of the mihrab, with its interesting fill-in motifs, is distinctly archaic. The presence of the numerous small specks of colour dotted over the field and main border is a feature usually associated with very early pieces, as this one certainly is. Note also the pleasing variations in shades of colour (abrash) which enliven the field and borders of the kilim.

PLATE 112

NORTH-EAST TURKEY PRAYER KILIM

Size: 182 x 135 cm.

Warp: Mostly white wool, one band of brown wool, one band of dark goat hair mixed with wool, S plied   32/10 cm.

Weft: Wool, S plied   180-220/10 cm.

Colours: Twelve – dark blue, light blue, greenish blue, aquamarine, red, brick red, salmon, straw, mauve, light brown, dark brown, ivory.

Technique: Slit-tapestry with a few extra brocade motifs.

Condition: Good – one end has had a slight repair.

By including deliberate shifts in colour and varying the design elements of both field and borders, the weaver of this kilim has succeeded in creating a fascinating textile which commands attention. It has the stamp of being the work of a very experienced weaver, and also one who took great pleasure in adding innovations as she proceeded. Even the use of varied materials for the warps sets this kilim apart from the mechanical appearance that some possess.

This kilim is possibly from the Bayburt-Gümüşhane area, to the north-west of this group of kilims.

PLATE 113

NORTH-EAST TURKEY TRIPLE-NICHE PRAYER KILIM

Size: 230 x 160 cm.

Warp: Wool, three strands of white, in some areas two strands of white and one dark brown, S plied   33/10 cm.

Weft: Wool, S plied   160/10 cm.

Colours: Nine – red (paler at one end), orange, yellow, turquoise, blue, straw, pale aubergine, dark brown, ivory.

Technique: Slit-tapestry with a few scattered brocade S motifs.

Condition: Good – the sides have been repaired.

Plates 113 and 114 illustrate two multiniche prayer kilims, or safs. The triple-niche prayer kilim is in exceptionally good condition for its age, and is beautifully constructed, using wool with a high lustre. Many prayer kilims retained their condition because they were never walked upon. So much skill and pride went into making them that often they were never used even for prayer; instead they were displayed only on occasions for special ceremonies. They are more a religious symbol, like certain holy pictures. It is for this reason that very old prayer kilims can sometimes be found which are still in excellent condition. We can recall the respect given in the past to prayer kilims by dealers generally. They would never walk on one, but nowadays, as the world has become more mercenary, the attitude adopted towards prayer kilims is less caring.

PLATE 114

NORTH-EAST TURKEY QUADRUPLE-NICHE PRAYER KILIM

Size: 282 x 140 cm.

Warp: Wool, one strand brown and one white, S plied   26/10 cm.

Weft: Wool, Z spun, mostly two strands used together; some plied   180/10 cm.

Colours: Ten – dark blue, pale blue, dark red, pale red, straw, yellow, pale mauve, turquoise, reddish brown, ivory.

Technique: Slit-tapestry weave.

Condition: It has had considerable repair; the sides and ends are restored.

This quadruple-niche prayer kilim is, without doubt, much older than the piece shown in plate 113. It probably dates from the beginning of the 19th century, or perhaps even earlier. Unfortunately, it has suffered somewhat, not from wear, but from a general disintegration of some of its fibre through sheer age. At some stage in its life someone has made some, frankly dreadful, attempts at repair. However, it is sufficiently complete and interesting to include it here. Note the glorious freedom with which the weaver has drawn each of the four mihrabs. The whole feeling of this kilim, including the design of the field and main border, gives an impression of great antiquity.

PLATE 115

NORTH-EAST TURKEY PRAYER KILIM

Size: 190 x 142 cm.

Warp: Wool, S plied   38/10 cm.

Weft: Wool, cotton in most white areas, S plied 220-240/10 cm.

Colours: Eleven – dark blue, pale blue, red, terracotta, green, blue-green, yellow, brown, maroon-brown, ivory, white (cotton).

Technique: Slit-tapestry weave with the remains of some contour weft wrapping.

Condition: Good.

The carefully executed weaving of the accompanying prayer kilim puts it in a different class. Using a design which has many similarities to that in plate 113, the weaver has developed it in her own way to compose a very interesting rug. At first glance it seems very precise and exact, but closer examination reveals numerous variations in the design. The resulting effect is far from static. It is woven using selected wools, skilfully spun and possessing a beautiful sheen. The areas of white cotton have become very matted with age. From its materials and colours we estimate that this kilim comes from the more westerly range of this group, possibly even as far west as Çankiri or Çorum.

PLATE 116

NORTH-EAST TURKEY KILIM

Size: 350 x 140 cm.

Warp: Wool, mostly orangy-brown, some greyish brown, a narrow band white, S plied   46/10 cm.

Weft: Wool, S plied   200-250/10 cm; also small amounts of metallic thread.

Colours: Thirteen – madder red, brownish red, dark blue, light blue, bluish green, turquoise, burnt orange, ochre, straw yellow, dark brown, reddish brown, salmon, ivory.

Technique: Slit-tapestry weave.

Condition: Excellent.

This is one of a pair of kilims obtained from a family who lived in Gümüşhane, due south of Trabzon, in north-east Turkey. The elderly brothers who offered them for sale claimed that they had inherited them from their grandmother but were very vague as to who could have made them. Whereas these two kilims, without doubt, were woven by the same person, the third piece they wanted to sell, from its colours, materials and design, obviously emanated further to the east and was of a type generally considered Kars-Kağizman in origin.

This kilim, in colouration and in the nature of its warps and wefting, has many similarities to that illustrated in plate 113. Kilims of this type are often attributed to the Bayburt district. Interestingly, Gümüşhane, lies fairly close to the town of Bayburt.

The beauty of this kilim rests in its richness of colour, combined with its fascinating design and attention to detail. As in plate 113, none of the motifs is outlined with supplementary wefts, a trait which distinguishes north-eastern kilims from the majority woven in Anatolia.

PLATE 117

NORTH-EAST TURKEY ÇUVAL

Size: 92 x 70 cm.

Warp: Brownish grey goat hair, as well as light brown wool and a wool-hair mixture, S plied   40/10 cm.

Weft: Wool, S plied in the design areas   220/10 cm; unplied Z spun in plain weave areas   140/10 cm; cotton is used for some white areas.

Colours: Ten – two blues, coral red, orange-red, orange, pale yellow, blue-green, reddish brown, ivory, white (cotton).

Technique: The face of the bag consists of bands of slit-tapestry figures separated by narrow stripes of modified zili (two-colour 1:1 floats); what remains of the back of the bag is made up of stripes of plain weft-faced weave in brown and red.

Condition: It is damaged at one end, but otherwise good.

Some of the design elements of this slit-tapestry woven çuval have similarities to pieces from other regions, but by the way its materials and colours have been used, this piece appears to have been made in these eastern parts of Turkey. The interaction of the white cotton and the more ivory-coloured wool, used together to surround some of the motifs, provides an interesting effect. Now that the materials are considerably aged, there is a distinct tonal difference between the white cotton and the more ivory-coloured wool. Although this bag face has suffered some damage to one end, it is still sufficiently complete to allow us to appreciate its pleasing design.

 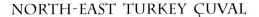

PLATE 118

ORDU PRAYER KILIM

Size: 170 x 134 cm.

Warp: Strong white wool, S plied   26/10 cm.

Weft: Wool, Z spun, cotton for white areas
140-220/10 cm.

Colours: Five – red, blue, yellow, brown, white (cotton).

Technique: Slit-tapestry weave.

Condition: Good.

With its robust weave, simple mihrab, lack of
borders and Spartan use of colours, this kilim
poses a bit of a puzzle. At first glance it might
be thought to be from the Erzerum-Bayburt
area, but the use of unplied wools for the wefting, among other things, would lead us to dis-
pense with this idea. Dealers with a good knowledge of kilims have variously ascribed it to the
Caucasus or the Erzerum area. Others have
stated it is from the Balkans, of the Manastir
type.

Certain aspects, in particular the character and
the spin of its wool, lead us to believe it is possibly from the Ordu region, from the mountainous tracts south of Samsun and Trabzon, near
the Black Sea. Design, colours and weave combine to make this a striking and effective
composition.

GLOSSARY

abrash: variegated bands in a colour, brought about by uneven dyeing of the wool.

brocade: a textile where each row of design wefts is followed by one or more shoots of ground weft.

cicim: a type of brocade used to produce motifs against a plain field (see text).

çuval: a storage bag usually decorated with kilim, soumak, zili or cicim. The most important decorative item in the nomad's tent.

elibelinde: a commonly employed motif described as hands on hips or arms akimbo.

gül: tribal emblem, usually in an octagonal form.

heybe: double bags or saddlebags. Like çuvals, they are woven using different techniques.

kilim: weft-faced flatweaves, usually slit-tapestry weaves in Turkey (see text).

lazy lines: small, stepped interstices in a block of colour caused by the weaver filling in small areas instead of working right across the colour zone. Common in kilims from north-east Turkey.

mihrab: in a prayer rug, the niche simulating the arch in a mosque which is directed towards Mecca.

soumak: a weft-wrapping technique used either in its pure form or as a brocade to produce decorative patterns (see text).

yastik: a cushion, like çuvals, woven using various techniques.

yayla: a high plateau, the grazing grounds for the nomads.

Yörük: Turkic nomads, with a seasonal migratory pattern ranging from summer mountain pastures to lowland plains for the winter months.

yürt: the circular tent made of felt used by tribal groups from Mongolia through to Turkey.

zili: a form of brocade where the design wefts are floated over and under varying numbers of warps (see text).

Z spun and S plied wool: since most spinners are right-handed, the wool is normally spun with a clockwise motion of the spindle. Consequently the fibres are twisted together in the direction of the slope of the letter Z. When two or more strands of spun wool are plied together, the twist of the ply needs to be opposite to that of the spin – thus a counterclockwise motion is normally employed. Looking at the plied yarn, the strands can be seen to lie in the direction of the slope of the shaft of the letter S.

NOTES ON THE
PRONUNCIATION OF TURKISH

We feel it is essential to point out some of the differences between the pronunciation of Turkish and English. Generally, Turkish is pronounced as it is written.

The letter c is pronounced like j in jam; but ç is pronounced like ch in church. Thus cicim ("jijim") and Çumra ("Chumra").

ş is pronounced like sh in shall. Thus Uşak ("Ushak").

The letter ğ normally lengthens the preceding vowel but is itself not pronounced; for example, Niğde ("Needeh"). The unaccented g is more or less as in English.

Sometimes o and u bear diaeresis marks. The pronunciation of ö is similar to u in fur, ü is pronounced as in the German *Führer*.

There are other exceptions, but the above points will enable the reader to come to grips with the pronunciation of most of the words and place-names used in this text.

NOTES ON THE
PHOTOGRAPHY

All photographs were taken by the authors on Ektachrome EPP120 film, using a Hasselblad 500C camera. Lighting was provided by two coupled electronic flash units. To obtain sufficient distance from them while trying to avoid parallax problems, we photographed the larger kilims from a ladder perched on top of our tractor shed. Photography was carried out at night-time so that the lighting could be controlled.

SELECTED BIBLIOGRAPHY

ACAR, BELKIS BALPINAR. 1983. *Kilim-Cicim-Zili-Sumak, Turkish Flatweaves.* Istanbul: Eren Yayinlari.

Anatolian Studies – Journal of British Archaeology at Ankara, 14. 1963.

ARFA, HASSAN. 1966. *The Kurds.* Oxford University Press.

ARKUS, LANDREAU, et al. 1978. *Yörük, The Nomadic Weaving Tradition of the Middle East.* Museum of Art, Carnegie Institute.

BALPINAR, B., and U. HIRSCH. 1982. *Flatweaves.* Wesel (Germany): Verlag Uta Hülsey.

BOIS, THOMAS. 1966. *The Kurds.* Beirut: Khayats.

CAHEN, CLAUDE. 1968. *Pre-Ottoman Turkey.* London: Sidgwick & Jackson.

D'ARCY, J.B. 1972. *Sheep Management and Wool Technology.* Sydney: NSW University Press.

BURR, MALCOLM. 1939. *The Insect Legion.* London: James Nisbet & Co. Ltd.

DER MANUELIAN, L., and M.L. EILAND. 1984. *Weavers, Merchants and Kings.* Fort Worth (USA): Kimbell Art Museum.

EDMONDS, C.J. 1957. *Kurds, Turks and Arabs.* Oxford University Press.

EYÜBOĞLU, U., I. OKAYGÜN, and F. YARAŞ. *Doğal Boyalari Yün Boyama.* Istanbul: Uygulamali Eğilim Vakfi.

GOODWIN, JILL. 1982. *A Dyer's Manual.* London: Pelham Books.

GROUSSET, RENÉ . 1948. *L'Empire des Steppes.* Paris: Payot.

JETTMAR, KARL. 1967. *Art of the Steppes.* New York: Crown Publishers.

KHLOPIN, I.N. The Manufacture of Pile Carpets in Bronze Age Central Asia. *Hali.* 5(2).

KENT, MARIAN. 1984. *The Great Powers and the End of the Ottoman Empire 1900-1923.* London: George Allen & Unwin.

LANDREAU, ANTHONY N., and W.R. PICKERING. 1969. *From the Bosporus to Samarkand – Flat-Woven Rugs.* Washington DC: The Textile Museum.

NIKITINE, B. 1956. *Les Kurdes, Étude Sociologique et Historique.* Paris: Imprimerie Nationale.

PETSOPOULOS, YANNI. 1979. *Kilims.* London: Thames & Hudson.

PEKIN, E. *Turkish Flatweaves and Carpets.* Istanbul: Minyatur Yayinlari.

ROUX, JEAN-PAUL. 1984. *Histoire des Turcs.* Mayard.

RUDENKO, SERGEI I. 1970. *Frozen Tombs of Siberia.* University of California Press.

SHAW, STANFORD J. 1976. *History of the Ottoman Empire and Modern Turkey.* Cambridge University Press.

SPIBEY, H. 1952. *The British Wool Manual.* Buxton (UK): Columbine Press.

TOYNBEE, A.J., and K.P. KIRKWOOD. 1926. *Turkey.* London.

VON BERGEN, WERNER. 1963. *Wool Handbook Volume I.* New York: Interscience Publishers.

INDEX